P9-CEP-441

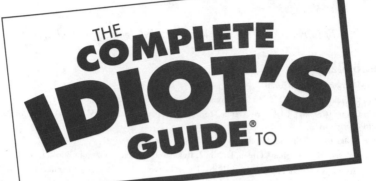
THE COMPLETE IDIOT'S GUIDE® TO

Designer Dogs

by Margaret H. Bonham

ALPHA

A member of Penguin Group (USA) Inc.

To Larry and to the Sky Warrior Sled Team, past and present.

ALPHA BOOKS

Published by the Penguin Group

Penguin Group (USA) Inc., 375 Hudson Street, New York, New York 10014, U.S.A.

Penguin Group (Canada), 10 Alcorn Avenue, Toronto, Ontario, Canada M4V 3B2 (a division of Pearson Penguin Canada Inc.)

Penguin Books Ltd, 80 Strand, London WC2R 0RL, England

Penguin Ireland, 25 St Stephen's Green, Dublin 2, Ireland (a division of Penguin Books Ltd)

Penguin Group (Australia), 250 Camberwell Road, Camberwell, Victoria 3124, Australia (a division of Pearson Australia Group Pty Ltd)

Penguin Books India Pvt Ltd, 11 Community Centre, Panchsheel Park, New Delhi—110 017, India

Penguin Group (NZ), cnr Airborne and Rosedale Roads, Albany, Auckland 1310, New Zealand (a division of Pearson New Zealand Ltd)

Penguin Books (South Africa) (Pty) Ltd, 24 Sturdee Avenue, Rosebank, Johannesburg 2196, South Africa

Penguin Books Ltd, Registered Offices: 80 Strand, London WC2R 0RL, England

International Standard Book Number: 1-59257-369-X
Library of Congress Catalog Card Number: 2005920508

03   04   05   8   7   6   5   4   3   2   1

Interpretation of the printing code: The rightmost number of the first series of numbers is the year of the book's printing; the rightmost number of the second series of numbers is the number of the book's printing. For example, a printing code of 05-1 shows that the first printing occurred in 2005.

Printed in the United States of America

Note: This publication contains the opinions and ideas of its author. It is intended to provide helpful and informative material on the subject matter covered. It is sold with the understanding that the author and publisher are not engaged in rendering professional services in the book. If the reader requires personal assistance or advice, a competent professional should be consulted.

The author and publisher specifically disclaim any responsibility for any liability, loss, or risk, personal or otherwise, which is incurred as a consequence, directly or indirectly, of the use and application of any of the contents of this book.

Most Alpha books are available at special quantity discounts for bulk purchases for sales promotions, premiums, fund-raising, or educational use. Special books, or book excerpts, can also be created to fit specific needs.

For details, write: Special Markets, Alpha Books, 375 Hudson Street, New York, NY 10014.

Publisher: *Marie Butler-Knight*
Product Manager: *Phil Kitchel*
Senior Managing Editor: *Jennifer Bowles*
Senior Acquisitions Editor: *Renee Wilmeth*
Development Editor: *Christy Wagner*
Senior Production Editor: *Billy Fields*

Copy Editor: *Jan Zoya*
Cartoonist: *Shannon Wheeler*
Cover/Book Designer: *Trina Wurst*
Indexer: *Tonya Heard*
Layout: *Angela Calvert*
Proofreading: *Mary Hunt*

Contents at a Glance

Contents

Introduction

You've heard about them on CNN. You've seen shows with these dogs on *National Geographic*. What are designer dogs? Are they mutts? Are they the next up-and-coming new breed? In this book, you learn a bit more about designer dogs—what they are and what they're not—and find out if there's a designer dog in your future.

Here you learn how genetics makes designer dogs into what they are and whether they're a *breed* or a *crossbreed*. I discuss the designers in depth and talk about the very best dog for your money. Scams abound with designer dogs, and many disreputable people are breeding these dogs without a thought of producing healthy and well-adjusted dogs. At the same time, good breeders are out there—you just have to find them.

What You'll Find in This Book

This book is intended for the first-time designer dog owner and also for owners of designer dogs who are interested in learning more about their dogs. It is divided into three user-friendly parts:

Part 1, "Are Designer Dogs in Your Future?" provides a basic overview of designer dogs and their personalities. It discusses the commitment required in designer dog ownership and whether the designer dog is right for you. I also discuss what a reputable breeder is and how to find the perfect designer dog for you. It explains vital health certifications and papers as well. Don't skip this part, as your choices will affect your dog's health and personality for years to come.

Part 2, "Bred by Design: A List of Designer Dogs," provides a basic overview of designer dogs—what's out there and what's available.

Part 3, "Living With Your Designer Dog," provides an overview of health issues, training, grooming, and safety and identification options for your designer dog. I also discuss the older designer dog and what to expect in his golden years.

Extras

Be sure to check out the sidebars throughout the book, too. They're packed full of fun and informative facts. Here's what to look for:

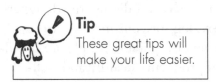

Tip
These great tips will make your life easier.

Did You Know?
And for some more interesting facts about dogs, check out these boxes.

Definition
Don't know what a word means? Check these definitions of terms used in this book.

Warning
Be sure to carefully read these warnings about possible problems that might arise with your designer dog.

Acknowledgments

A huge thanks to the following people for their support: Jessica Faust, Bookends—top-notch agent; Mike Sanders—for the recommendation; Renee Wilmeth, senior acquisitions editor; Christy Wagner, development editor; Billy Fields, senior production editor; and Beth Adelman, technical editor.

A huge thanks for photos from Diane Peters Mayer and Benny the Bagel; Ken Fischer and Aussie (Labradoodle); Lori Herrold and Flint and Fiona (Labradoodle); Earl A. Gershenow and Solly (Labradoodle); Debbie Cowdrey and Tanner and Rusty; LT/COL Mary D. Foley, USA (Ret) and Panda; Bonnie Wagenbach and her adorable Yorkipoos and Poochons; Shirley Kitelinger and her adorable Maltipoos; Jean Fogel; Mai Idzkowski and the Nike Animal Rescue Foundation (NARF; narfrescue.org) and Daisy Mae; Hilary Lane and Wally; Renee Pierce, Pierce Schnoodles; and the Rocky Mountain Border Collie Rescue.

Other thanks go to The North American Cockapoo Club; the International Labradoodle Association; and the Rocky Mountain Border Collie Rescue (www.rockymountainbcrescue.org/) for their help.

Special Thanks to the Technical Reviewer

The Complete Idiot's Guide to Designer Dogs was reviewed by an expert who double-checked the accuracy of what you'll learn here, to help us ensure that this book gives you everything you need to know about designer dogs. Special thanks are extended to Beth Adelman. Beth grew up with dogs and is a former editor of the *AKC Gazette* and *DogWorld* magazine and the online magazine, TheDogDaily.com. She has been involved in publishing books and magazines about companion animals for more than 15 years.

Trademarks

All terms mentioned in this book that are known to be or are suspected of being trademarks or service marks have been appropriately capitalized. Alpha Books and Penguin Group (USA) Inc. cannot attest to the accuracy of this information. Use of a term in this book should not be regarded as affecting the validity of any trademark or service mark.

Part 1

Are Designer Dogs in Your Future?

Designer dogs. Crossbreeds. Hybrids. Designer mutts. You've heard of them by a dozen different names, and you're wondering what those cute dogs are and why they have such a big price tag. Are they purebreds? Are they mutts? What are they exactly?

Maybe you know a little about designer dogs and are wondering if one might be right for you. Or perhaps you suffer from allergies and still want a dog that you can have fun with.

In Part 1, you learn what designer dogs are. I look at the claims about designer dogs and explain whether they're true or not. I also show you how to find the very best designer dog for you and your family.

(Photo courtesy of Bonnie Wagenbach)

What Are Designer Dogs?

In This Chapter

- Learning what designer dogs really are
- Understanding the appeal of designer dogs
- Looking at the common designer dog breeds

You might have heard about designer dogs in the news or seen them on TV. Your neighbor might have one—and paid $2,500 and had him shipped from Australia. Maybe you heard that designer dogs make the best pets or are great if you have allergies. Or perhaps you think you want to get one for your family, but you're not sure about all you've heard. What are designer dogs exactly, and are these dogs worth the price tag the breeders are demanding?

In this chapter, I talk about what designer dogs are and, just as important, what they are *not*. I also cover why designer dogs are popular and discuss some of the beneficial claims about these dogs.

The Development of Designer Dogs

The history of the dog is indeed ancient. Experts argue about when dogs were domesticated, but most cite archaeological evidence and place domestication at 20,000 years ago; DNA evidence suggests it was as long as 125,000 years ago. If you look at the history of many dog breeds, most were developed by crossing previously known breeds. In fact, a May 21, 2004, article in *Science Magazine* claims that only nine breeds come from the original ancient stock and the rest of the purebreds have been developed in the last 300 years from these breeds and breeds that no longer exist. Many of the purebreds we recognize today were developed intentionally from other breeds. The Doberman Pinscher, for example, originated around 1890 and was a blend of Rottweiler, Black and Tan Terrier, and smooth-hair German Pinscher and was recognized as a breed in Germany by the 1900s. At one point or another, most purebreds were "designer dogs."

Did You Know?

Some designer cross-breeds have been around a long time; others have not. Cockapoos and Peekapoos have been in existence since the 1950s.

In many cases, dogs such as the Labradoodle, the Cockapoo, and the Schnoodle are being bred not only purebred to purebred (i.e., Labrador Retriever to Poodle, Cocker Spaniel to Poodle, or Schnauzer to Poodle) but also Labradoodle to Labradoodle, Cockapoo to Cockapoo, or Schnoodle to Schnoodle.

How it all started was probably an accident: a breeder of two breeds had an unplanned breeding. With that litter, the breeder discovered she had a dog who had an *open coat* and the best qualities of both breeds—a crossbreed that would make a fine pet. Perhaps those first "accidents" were giveaways, but soon the market for crossbreeds developed as more people wanted these specific mixes.

Could it have been planned? Maybe, but many crossbreed breeders agree the history is murky and most likely the original litters were unplanned.

At some point, a few breeders started incorrectly calling cross-bred dogs "rare breeds" and demanding high prices for them because of their "rarity." Cockapoos, Peekapoos, and other cross-breeds fell into disfavor with the dog world because many of their breeders were out to make money and not necessarily to produce a healthy dog. Many reputable purebred breeders warned against buy-ing these "rare breeds" because these dogs weren't tested for diseases and were often produced in *puppy mill* conditions. (At some point, some breeders recognized that their dogs suffered from some of the same afflictions as their purebred counterparts and began screening for diseases. More on how breeders screen for diseases later.)

Definition _____

Dogs with a **single coat** have a coat that has no undercoat and does not have yearly or twice-yearly shedding (hair does come out much as human hair). Dogs with an **open coat** have a type of single coat, but it's normally less thick. **Puppy mills** are places where dogs are produced commercially where the bottom line is to make money, not to produce a quality dog.

But the allure of the specialized crossbred still existed. People loved the look of many of the mixes and wanted a dog who would be a good companion. To get the kind of dog they wanted, people were willing to pay good money.

In more recent times, guide dog groups such as Canine Com-panions for Independence crossbred dogs such as Golden Retrievers and Labrador Retrievers to develop a more tractable guide dog that has the positive characteristics from both breeds. Labradoodles were actually developed for guide-dog work for people with allergies because their open coat was less likely to trigger allergic reactions than the Labrador Retriever's double coat.

Why Designer Dogs Are So Popular

Designer dogs are popular for many reasons, such as their health and their *single coats* that some people with allergies can tolerate (see the "The 'Hybrid' Vigor" and "The Hypoallergenic Claims" sections later in this chapter), but hype plays a role, too. Designer dogs are cool and have cute-sounding names to go with the dog: Labradoodle, Goldendoodle, Cockapoo, and who wouldn't want a Schnoodle? (See the following "Common Mixes" section for more names.) Attach a high price tag, and voilà, you've got a trendy dog.

Did You Know? _____

Many city dwellers want a small dog but find few small mixed breeds at animal shelters. Coupled with the reluctance of some rescue groups and shelters to place even a small dog with someone who lives in an apartment, many people turn to a designer dog bred to be a small companion pet.

Some breeders claim that designer dogs are easier to train than other breeds. Although certain designer dogs might be smart and trainable, the crossbreeding leaves the trainability issue questionable because you're dealing with many genetic components (see Chapter 2). Designer dogs are still dogs and do require effort in training. Anyone claiming that designer dogs are more trainable and smarter than purebred dogs is misleading buyers.

The "Hybrid" Vigor

The designer crossbreed has become popular in the recent years because of the obvious health problems associated with purebreds. Open any one of the many books out there about purebred dogs, and you'll find that authors (this author included) warn of potential health problems associated with poorly bred dogs of every breed.

Even if the dog is well bred, most purebreds have the genetic potential for many inherited diseases, such as *hip dysplasia, progressive retinal atrophy,* and cardiac problems that can crop up even in the most conscientious breeder's lines. For example, according to the Association of Veterinarians for Animal Rights, the German Shepherd Dog has 82 known hereditary diseases lurking in the breed's gene pool, the Labrador Retriever has 54, and the Toy Poodle has 51.

No doubt, pet buyers have also heard that mixed breeds are healthier and less prone to temperament problems. This is only partially true. Going to a breeder who screens for diseases such as hip dysplasia will actually reduce your chances of obtaining a sick dog, regardless of whether the dog is a purebred or a mixed breed.

Definition _____

Hip dysplasia is a hereditary disease that causes hip-joint malformation. **Progressive retinal atrophy** is a hereditary disease that leads to blindness in dogs.

Mixed breed proponents have often claimed that mutts and crossbreeds are naturally healthier, citing "hybrid vigor." This is a difficult statement to define, but most people mean that by widening the gene pool, there's less chance for a disease to crop up. In theory, this is a good idea. However, in many breeds, the potential for the same genetic disease still exists. Although mixed breeds are less apt to have certain genetic diseases prevalent only in certain breeds, some diseases appear in dogs of every breed (or mix of breeds) because they are diseases of the species, namely, *canis lupus familiaris,* or the dog.

But are designer dogs healthier? It really depends. Remember that beneath it all, dogs are still dogs, and they might or might not inherit bad genes from their parents. If two of the same bad recessive genes crop up, you may have a sick dog.

> **Did You Know?** _____
> Hereditary diseases aren't just because of inbreeding, but because of poor breeding practices. Although inbreeding does double up on genes (both good and bad), poor breeding practices such as breeding dogs with hereditary defects are more likely to cause health problems than just inbreeding alone. This is why breeders must screen their dogs for genetic problems through either genetic testing or health tests.

The Hypoallergenic Claims

One of the biggest reasons for buying a designer dog often has to do with the hypoallergenic claim. Many designer dogs have Poodle in them and have inherited the relatively shed-free single coat—better for people with allergies or who don't want dog hair all over—making these dogs quite popular. Many breeders claim these dogs won't affect allergies, and in talking to some people who have allergies, it appears that they might be less affected by less hair and dander.

But there's no silver bullet here. Often people are allergic to the dog's saliva, not just to the dander and the hair. A person with allergies can have a reaction to a "hypoallergenic" dog.

> **Tip** _____
> If you have allergies, talk with your allergist about getting a dog and what you can do to mitigate the effect of the allergies. (Medications can help!) If your allergist is strictly a "no dog" or "outside dog only" doctor, you might have to get a second opinion or perhaps choose not to get a dog, especially if your allergies are severe.

As a general rule, it's a bad idea to purchase a dog based on hypoallergenic claims alone. I've known people who could tolerate certain breeds of dogs and not others. If you're allergic to dogs already, the best thing you can do is visit a breeder and spend a day with the dogs. Or if you have a friend with one, see if she'll "loan" you her dog for a day to see how well you tolerate him.

Common Mixes

Let's look at a rundown of some of the most common designer dogs:

- Labradoodles = Labrador Retrievers + Poodles
- Goldendoodles = Golden Retrievers + Poodles
- Cockapoos (or Cockerpoos or Spoodles) = Cocker Spaniels + Poodles
- Peekapoos = Pekingeses + Poodles
- Schnoodles (or Snoodles) = Schnauzers + Poodles
- Yorkipoos = Yorkshire Terriers + Poodles
- Sheltipoos = Shetland Sheepdogs + Poodles
- Maltipoos = Maltese + Poodles
- Shihpoos (or Pooshihs) = Shih Tzu + Poodles
- Bassadoodles = Basset Hounds + Poodles
- Border Collie Terriers = Border Collies + Jack Russell Terriers—note this is not the AKC breed!
- Border Shepherds = Border Collies + German Shepherd Dogs or Australian Shepherds
- Border Retrievers = Border Collies + Labrador Retrievers or Golden Retrievers
- Alaskan Huskies = Siberian Huskies + Alaskan Malamutes + Lurchers
- Scandinavian Hounds = English Setters + German Shorthair Pointers
- Golden Labradors = Golden Retrievers + Labrador Retrievers

- Dorgis = Dachshunds + Pembroke Corgis or Cardigan Corgis
- Bagels = Beagles + Basset Hounds
- Chihchons = Chihuahuas + Bichons Frises
- Shihchons = Shih Tzus + Bichons Frises
- Pugles = Pugs + Beagles
- Bull Boxers = Bull Dogs + Boxers
- Bi-Tzus = Bichons Frises + Shih Tzus

Tip

Designer dogs are produced primarily due to public demand, so depending on what breeds are popular, the designer crossbreed will be, too. But don't settle on just one crossbreed because you've heard of it. Try to meet as many designer dog types as you can and you'll get a better understanding what the differences are.

The "Poo" Dogs—Poodle Mixes

The most common dogs in the designer dog breeding are the Poodle crossbreeds. These dogs can come in small, medium, and large, depending on whether a Toy, Mini, or Standard Poodle was used in the cross. These crosses typically take the nonshed, open coats and the intelligence of the Poodle and combine those qualities with the personality of the breed it's crossed with.

Miniatures and Miniature Mixes

Miniature crossbreeds include the Bichon Frise mixes, Bassett Hound mixes, Pug mixes, and Dachshund mixes. Like the Poodle crosses, the Bichon Frise crosses are intended to produce a dog with an open coat.

In cases where the breed has health problems due to brachycephalic heads, long bodies, or other issues, the cross is often done to provide a healthier dog.

Other Crossbreeds

Besides the Poo dogs and Miniatures, you'll notice other crossbreeds listed here. Some are working crossbreeds such as the Alaskan Husky and Scandinavian Hound. Other crosses are for performance reasons, such as the Border Collie Terrier, Border Retriever, or Golden Labrador, who all excel in agility and flyball. Still others are interesting crosses that breeders couldn't resist, or perhaps were an accident that proved to be fortuitous.

Warning

Some breeds such as Poodles and Golden Retrievers have inherited skin problems. Ask the breeder if he's seen any skin problems with his dogs and if he breeds dogs with skin problems.

Crossbreeds That Don't Work

Not all crossbreeds are a good idea. Some breeds have serious health problems that could be exacerbated by adding another breed. For example, breeding a Pug and a English Toy Spaniel could cause more problems with eyes and breathing—two common problems with severely brachycephalic dogs—as well as patellar luxation (slipping kneecaps), Legg-Calve-Perthes disease (a serious hip problem), and other joint problems.

The Least You Need to Know

- Designer dogs are not a breed, but a group of specialized crossbreeds who were bred mainly for companion purposes.

- Designer dogs have been around a long while—from the time people took two breeds and created a crossbreed for a specific purpose. Most designer dogs are recent, but a few, like the Cockapoo, have been around since the 1950s.

Designer dogs are popular for a variety of reasons: they're trendy, they offer a choice for someone who wants a specialized dog but not a purebred, and they're healthy and sometimes hypoallergenic pets.

A Closer Look at Designer Dogs

In This Chapter

- 🏠 Making a designer dog: a little doggie genetics
- 🏠 First-generation or generational: deciding what's best for you
- 🏠 Determining if designer dogs are better than purebreds
- 🏠 Understanding what you get in a designer dog

To make an informed decision when purchasing your designer dog, you need to understand a bit more about dog breeds and genetics. In this chapter, I cover the common designer dogs. Some you've probably heard of, and some you probably haven't. Regardless, there's bound to be one to suit your fancy.

The Genetics of the Dog

To understand the designer dog, you must first understand genetics. The dog has 78 chromosomes, divided into 39 pairs. Of those 39 pairs, 38 are *autosomal*, or non-sex-related chromosomes. One pair contains the sex chromosomes, either XX (female) or XY (male).

In these chromosomes is the dog's DNA. From the tiniest Chihuahua to the largest Great Dane and everything in between, all dogs are dogs because of their DNA. When two dogs mate, each parent gives half of his or her chromosomes to the new puppy, which means that the pup gets some characteristics from her mother and some from his father. Which characteristics are passed on is a random chance in every individual pup.

Genes that sit in the same position on the chromosome but that may affect traits differently are called *alleles*. If the alleles are the same for a certain trait, they are *homozygous* for that trait. If the alleles are different, they are *heterozygous*. Depending on whether the genes are dominant or recessive, the dog could be a carrier for a trait that doesn't appear outwardly.

 Definition _____

Non-sex-related genes are autosomal. **Alleles** are genes that occupy the same position on the chromosome and govern traits but may be different in how they affect traits. Two alleles that are the same or match up are **homozygous.** Two different alleles are **heterozygous.** If one is recessive, the dog will not have the trait expressed by that gene, but will be a carrier for the trait and could pass it on to his or her offspring. A **hybrid** is a cross between two species or two varieties within a species.

When Austrian botanist Gregor Mendel crossed tall and short pea plants in the 1850s, he found that the height characteristics did not average out in later generations, but rather, that some plants were tall and some were short. He hypothesized that the plants had certain characteristics that were passed on to their offspring, and these characteristics were either dominant or recessive. When crossing *hybrid* plants of different (heterozygous) heights, Mendel discovered a 3-to-1 ratio: one plant would have two dominant alleles (and would show the dominant trait); two plants would have a dominant and a recessive allele (and would show the dominant trait but be able to pass on the recessive trait to their offspring); and one plant would have two recessive alleles (and would show the recessive trait). Of course, this is a perfect mathematical model, and it only describes the *likelihood* of something happening.

But what about dogs? Surely they're more complex than peas? Indeed, they are. Many traits in dogs are controlled not by just one gene, but by many. However, Mendel's basic rules do apply when dealing with the most basic genes, even in dogs.

How Purebreds Are Made

The total genetic makeup of a dog is known as the *genotype*. Before we learned the genotype makeup of dog breeds, we had to rely on the *phenotype*, or the outward appearance of the dog. But now we know that because of recessive genes, a dog can carry a trait that doesn't show on the outside. Enter the canine genome project, which has mapped the canine genes.

Did You Know? _____
To learn more about the Canine Genome Project, go to mendel.berkeley.edu/dog.html.

We now know from DNA evidence that dogs originally descended from Asian wolves (not coyotes, jackals, or any other wild canid). Plenty of theories exist on how the dog became domesticated. Some believe that dogs were self-domesticating— those wolves who hung around the *Homo sapiens*'s garbage pits were more likely to accept humans than their wild counterparts. Others

Definition _____
The genetic makeup of a dog is called its genotype. The physical traits you can see in a dog due to the **genotype** and the environment are called the **phenotype**. The retention of immature or puppy-like qualities into adulthood is called **neoteny**.

believe humans possibly had a hand in domesticating the Asian wolf. Regardless of which theory you subscribe to, traits such as *neoteny*, flopped ears, and spots seem to come with domestication and may be closely aligned with the domestication genes.

Early people chose the dogs they wanted to have with them for a variety of reasons. Some needed dogs who could hunt well; others needed dogs who would bond closely to and guard herds. People didn't know about genetics, but they did know what they wanted in a dog, so they bred the dogs who had the characteristics they were looking for. As people continued to breed dogs, certain traits and even mutations (genetic differences that occur randomly) began to appear, many of which were recessive genes linked to domestication. Sometimes the new variation was selected because it made sense for the work the dog was doing, such as the coat length, thickness, or even color; other traits were selected simply because people liked them, such as the short muzzle seen on dogs such as Boxers and Bulldogs.

But this isn't the only way breeds have formed. Some breeds were intentionally created by a handful of breeders who were look-ing to produce a dog for a specific purpose. In some cases, certain breeds came about because of the work of one man or woman who saw a particular dog who was so exceptional that the person wanted to create more dogs like him. The breeder then established a careful breeding program and usually kept good records, thus creating a new breed out of dogs that fit his or her criteria.

What Happens When You Crossbreed

When you take two dogs of different breeds, you combine the genes of those two breeds. But the genetic differences between breeds are very small, even if the outward appearances might be very great. All dogs are still the same species and their genes still make them dogs. When you breed two different breeds, such as the Labrador

Retriever and the Poodle, you're still breeding two dogs, no matter how dissimilar they look. Any alleles those two breeds share will create a dog with homozygous traits. This can be good or bad, depending on the traits.

For example, if you breed a dog who has an open coat with a dog of another breed with an open coat, it's very unlikely that you'll produce a dog with a double coat; you'll very likely get one with an open coat. Likewise, if you breed a dog with a recessive gene for a particular color to a dog with a recessive gene for the same color, you might end up with a puppy with that recessive color. This occurs with genetic diseases as well: breed a dog with a health problem and you're likely to get either a sick dog or a carrier. But the recessive diseases are also there: breed two healthy dogs who both have the recessive gene for a disease, and you are likely to get a dog with the disease.

The dog might have traits more like one of the parents than the other, or it might have a blending of both parents. However, dog genetics is complex and doesn't always rely on one allele per trait, so you're likely to see a dog who looks somewhere in between both parents.

How Designer Dogs Are Made

Is breeding designer dogs more than just getting dogs from two different breeds and breeding them? Yes and no. In some circumstances, breeders get and breed purebreds and then sell first-generation designer breeds. Assuming that the breeder is reputable (more on reputable breeders in Chapter 4), the breeder will screen the parents for genetic diseases and for desirable personality traits. If the breeder is committed to breeding that particular designer dog, he or she might establish a multi-generational breeding program and continue producing dogs.

First Generation Versus Generational

A first-generation crossbreed dog is a dog who is the product of two purebred dogs, A generational dog is a dog who is the product of two crossbred dogs of first generation or generational crossbreeds. So what's better, a first-generation or a generational dog? It's really a matter of taste and what's important to you. Here are some points to keep in mind:

- Generational dogs are more likely to be more consistent in looks and personality than first-generation dogs.

- First-generation dogs might have undesirable traits from dominant genes that either parent may have, such as a coat that isn't quite right, or may look more like one parent than the other.

- First-generation dogs are more likely to have more health benefits, assuming that the parents of the dogs were cleared for diseases (that is certified through OFA, CERF, or another registry that the dog was found free from certain hereditary diseases).

- Generational dogs may have recessive genes show up from either breed of the original crossbreed, producing a trait you didn't want or you didn't know you'd get.

- Generational dogs may have a disease that crops up in either breed that wouldn't appear in a first-generation dog.

- Either dog is quite capable of being a loving companion, so unless you're looking for a specific look or trait in your designer dog (such as an open coat or the drive for a certain sport or activity), any dog you choose will be a good friend.

> **Tip**
>
> Ask the breeder if he or she breeds generational or first-generation dogs and why. Most reputable breeders have their reasons for doing either.

Are Designer Dogs a Breed?

The short answer is no. Designer dogs aren't registered with American Kennel Club (AKC), United Kennel Club (UKC), or any of the other reputable purebred registries, because breeding two purebred dogs from different breeds doesn't make a breed. Breeding first-generation dogs to other designer dogs doesn't make a breed, either.

A designer dog is a crossbreed. Some might say it's a very expensive mutt, and that isn't far from the truth. However, the designer dog is purposely bred for qualities that make up that crossbreed. In most cases, these dogs are bred for companionship, but in a few cases, the dogs are bred for specific types of work or competition.

What Makes a Breed?

Being registered with a particular kennel club such as the AKC or UKC doesn't necessary define a breed, but it does help. Most breeds in the United States are recognized by these registries under some very strict standards. For example, the AKC board of directors must determine if there is commitment to the breed. This requires a national breed club that writes and oversees the *breed standard*, maintains the *studbook*, and holds *specialties* with a minimum of 100 active households who show, work, breed, and otherwise advance the breed. It requires that all dogs have three-generation backgrounds and that all the dogs in that *pedigree* be of the same pure breed. The breed must be well established by the time the breed club applies for registration, with at least 300 to 400 dogs in 20 or more states. The AKC also looks at the purpose of the dog, or what the dog was originally bred to do and how that dog has become specialized toward that purpose.

With purebreds, generally you can't leave the studbook open (allow breeding of unregistered dogs) for unregistered dogs to add to the population of registered dogs (not without the approval of the national kennel club and only in special conditions). Crossing in new stock from other breeds isn't allowed, either.

> **Definition**
>
> The breed standard is a description of the ideal dog of each breed and is the standard by which all dogs in the breed are judged. Dogs within a certain breed must mostly conform to the breed standard or risk being disqualified. The breed standard is what distinguishes each dog breed from all the others. A studbook is a list of purebred dogs registered within a breed who were bred and produced puppies. A specialty is a specialized conformation dog show in which only dogs within the same breed are allowed to compete. The family tree of a dog is called a pedigree.

If first-generation designer dogs can't be considered a breed, can those from multiple generations? If designer dog breeders were to get together and form a national breed club, establish a standard, maintain a studbook, and, at some time, close the studbook to dogs from new stock (thus maintaining a pure breed), then that particular designer dog may be able to cross into the realm of a breed and no longer be considered a crossbreed. As we mentioned in Chapter 1, that's how many well-established breeds today were originally formed.

Purebreds Versus Crossbreeds

Just because a designer dog is a crossbreed doesn't make it inferior to a purebred. As a pet, a designer crossbreed might be perfect for you and your situation. However, there are some distinct differences between owning a purebred and a designer crossbreed that you should be aware of:

🏠 A registered purebred will have "papers" with an established registry such as the AKC or UKC. The dog's offspring can also be registered, provided the dog is bred with another registered purebred of the same breed.

🏠 A purebred will be able to compete in "dog shows," that is, *conformation shows* and *performance events*. (Dogs who are considered mixed breeds can compete in performance events not sanctioned by the AKC.)

A purebred will have a known look and personality. While those who breed designer crossbreeds strive for a homogenous look, some dogs won't quite fit the look and personality the breeder was trying to achieve.

 Definition
A conformation show is a dog show at which dogs are judged according to how well they conform to a standard. During performance events, dogs compete for titles in areas such as obedience, agility, tracking, rally, and herding.

If these points are important to you, you should not consider a crossbreed dog. However, if you are looking for a family pet, a designer crossbreed might be in your future.

Did You Know?
An AKC-registered purebred has his pedigree on file at the AKC, which proves that the dog comes from purebred stock. An unregistered purebred has no pedigree on file (or nothing to reference that pedigree) and even though he might look like a purebred, he might actually have other breeds in his lineage.

Beyond the Price Tag: What Are You Getting for Your Money?

One look at the price tag for designer dogs and you might think twice about getting one. After all, some designer dogs cost more than purebreds.

If you purchase a dog from a reputable breeder (more on reputable breeders in Chapter 4), you're paying for a proven product—a dog who has been carefully bred and genetically screened to provide the healthiest pet you can possibly get.

But aren't these dogs mutts? Yes, technically they are. But they're mutts with a special pedigree, which means you know what you're getting. When you look at the common mixed breeds you see in animal shelters, you can't be 100 percent sure of what breeds are in them nor whether their parents were of a good temperament. Their random breeding is what separates them from intentionally crossbred designer dogs.

 Warning

Price is not indicative of quality when it comes to a designer dog. Although designer dogs are expensive, some breeders charge a higher price because that's what the market will bear. Most reputable breeders charge a price that helps pay for their time, genetic testing, veterinary bills, and other puppy-related costs.

The Least You Need to Know

- Designer dogs can inherit both good and bad qualities from their parent breeds.

- Designer dogs aren't true hybrids in terms of interspecies breeding because they're still a breeding between dogs.

- First-generation designer dogs might have less consistency and might look more like one parent than the other.

- Generational designer dogs might look more consistent, but they are more likely to display recessive characteristics or genetic diseases found in either breed.

Chapter

3

Finding the Right Designer Dog for You

In This Chapter

- Deciding if you really want a dog
- Finding the right designer dog or puppy for you
- Learning where you should—and *should not*— get a designer dog

If you're still deciding whether a designer dog is right for you, this chapter will help you to make a decision. We will look at some of the responsibilities of owning a dog—including some you may not have thought of. Then we consider different designer dogs and help you choose the right one for you and your lifestyle: puppy or adult? Regular or supersize? Does the dog have a high or low activity level? All this is important if you want the dog to fit with you and your family.

You'll also find out where to get your designer dog—and just as important, where *not* to.

Reality Check: Do You Really Want a Dog?

Before you decide a designer dog is really for you and your family, take a step back and do a reality check. As wonderful as a designer dog may be, a designer dog is still a dog—with all the inconveniences and responsibilities that go along with owning a dog.

Sadly, a number of people buy a designer dog as their first dog, not realizing the responsibility that comes with pet ownership. Your designer dog will require food, water, shelter, exercise, and attention *every day*, in addition to routine veterinary care, training, and grooming. Puppies require even more commitment from you: constant attention, housetraining (they don't come housetrained!), and obedience training.

Warning

All dogs need attention, so if you're not able to spend time with a pet, get a houseplant!

Most designer dogs were developed to be pets. They require more attention than a lot of other dogs, so it's important for you to decide whether a designer dog will fit into your busy lifestyle now, before you purchase a puppy or an adult dog. If you don't have a single minute to yourself, how are you going to have time for a pet?

Before you bring home a designer dog, consider the following:

- A healthy designer dog will live, on average, 10 to 15 years. Are you willing to rearrange your lifestyle to accommodate an animal that is dependent solely on you for that length of time?

- Are you able to financially afford to care for your pet? The cost of a puppy does not end at its purchase price. Your designer puppy—and dog—will require ongoing food and veterinary expenses throughout its life. Puppies and elderly dogs will generally incur more expenses than adult dogs.

- Does everyone in the household want a dog? All members of the family must agree on a new pet.

🏠 Is anyone in your family allergic to dogs? Don't purchase a designer dog hoping that maybe the person with allergies will be able to tolerate him. Have the allergic person visit someone who owns the breed of designer dog you're considering for your family to see if the dog sets off his or her allergies.

🏠 Who will take care of your dog? An adult in the household must take responsibility for the dog. As much as they love the dog, children cannot be depended on to take care of a living, breathing animal.

🏠 If you have a backyard, is it fenced in, dig-proof, climb-proof, and jump-proof?

🏠 Are you willing to take your designer dog for a walk each day, as well as give him some other exercise every day?

🏠 Are you willing to go to obedience classes to train and socialize a puppy?

🏠 Are you able to get home to your designer dog every 9 hours or less (far more frequently when that dog is a puppy)? If not, are you able to hire a pet-sitter to walk him?

🏠 Are you able to give your dog attention every day?

🏠 Are you willing to put up with muddy paw prints on your clothing and carpets?

🏠 What about dog hair? Although many designer dogs are low-shed and don't shed their undercoat, they still do lose some hair.

🏠 Are you able to tolerate the destructiveness associated with a dog? Puppies and dogs might chew on the wrong things or dig in the flowerbed. Puppies don't come housetrained, and the adult dog may have an occasional accident.

🏠 Are you able to make plans for your dog when you go on vacation or on a business trip?

🏠 Do you have other commitments you might have to fulfill
(such as college, armed forces, etc.) that might leave you
scrambling to take care of your dog?

If you've never owned a dog before, you might look at these
questions and wonder whether I'm exaggerating the responsibilities
of dog ownership. I'm not. Unfortunately, too many people purchase a dog without realizing the basic owner responsibilities. Be
an informed dog owner. You and your dog will be happier for it!

Which Designer Dog Is Right for Your Lifestyle?

You might be wondering which crossbreed will work best for you.
Look at the crossbreed chapters in Part 2. Some will appeal to you
more than others; make a list of those dogs you like. Then think
carefully about the dogs, your lifestyle, and your list of preferences.
Ask yourself the following questions:

🏠 Do you want a smart dog who is very trainable?

🏠 Do you have the need for low shedding?

🏠 Do you have the time to groom a dog?

🏠 Are you active and want your dog to be active with you?

🏠 Are you a homebody?

🏠 Do you live in an apartment?

🏠 Do you have a backyard?

🏠 Do you have time to exercise an energetic dog?

🏠 Do you have a disability?

🏠 Are you elderly?

🏠 Do you want a calm or an energetic dog?

🏠 Do you have children?

🏠 Do you have other pets?

🏠 Is this your first dog?

🏠 Do you want an independent dog or one who likes to be around you?

🏠 Do you have allergies?

The type of designer dog who will fit in your life depends on these and other questions. For example, if you are elderly or have a disability, a large, rambunctious puppy might cause problems for you. Likewise, if you live in an apartment, a small or toy crossbreed might be better than a large or medium-size dog. If you're not the active type, look for a low-activity dog. If you're active, get a dog who can keep up with you and participate in your activities as well. Having a fenced-in backyard is good for larger dogs or dogs who need a lot of exercise. If you already have pets, getting a dog who is good with other animals is also a good idea.

Warning

A puppy younger than 6 months old has a small bladder and can't "hold it" for longer than 4 hours a day. If you go to work or school during the day, you must go home and exercise your puppy around lunchtime and again right after work or school. If you're unable to do this, hire a professional dog-sitter.

Considerations When Getting a Designer Dog

Most people choose the cutest puppy they see. But there's more to picking a dog than just getting the cute one who "chooses you." Keeping in mind your lifestyle and preferences (see the preceding section), let's look at some other choices you have to make.

Puppy or Adult?

A large percentage of pet buyers are usually puppy buyers because puppies are so cute. At 8 weeks old, the puppy doesn't have bad habits ingrained yet, and you get to watch the puppy grow up.

That being said, puppies are a handful. They're not house-trained. They're not socialized. They haven't a clue what the rules of the house are and quite often make up their own. They chew inappropriate items. And they need training.

Be honest with yourself and your time constraints before purchasing a puppy. If you don't have the time to spend on your puppy's training (including going to professional obedience training classes), exercising, and socializing, maybe a puppy isn't the best choice for you.

Adult dogs are usually housetrained or will housetrain in a very short amount of time. Adults are a bit more "settled" and less active than puppies and might even know a few commands or tricks. And when it comes to looks, there are no surprises with adults—what you see is what you get. On the negative side, adults might have learned a few bad habits and might need some training to unlearn those bad habits.

Did You Know?
Adult dogs will bond to you as well as a young puppy will, provided you spend time with them. The level of bonding has more to do with the amount of time you spend training, socializing, and just being with your dog.

Remember, these crossbreeds usually live to be more than 10 and sometimes even more than 15 years old. An adult dog still has many good years ahead of him.

Male or Female?

For the most part, gender is a personal preference, as both males and females make excellent pets. If you're a first-time dog owner, a female might be a better choice because female dogs are less likely to test you.

In some breeds, females tend to be more dependent and males more independent. In other breeds, the opposite is true. You can't make these assumptions with crossbreeds, so be ready to rely on personality tests to determine which puppy or dog is right for you.

Male or female, you should spay or neuter your dog. Spaying, or removing the female's reproductive organs generally costs more than neutering and is a major surgery compared to neutering. However, a good veterinarian who has performed spays routinely shouldn't have any problems spaying your dog.

Tiny, Small, Medium, Large, or Supersize?

Size does matter—especially with dogs. You probably already have a preference, but before you decide on a particular size, consider the following:

- 🏠 Toy, small, and medium-size dogs are good for apartment dwellers or people with limited strength or lower activity levels. They're also good for people with small yards.

- 🏠 Medium and large dogs can be intimidating to strangers and may make a person living alone feel more secure. Of course, on the flip side, some people are so intimidated by a large dog that they don't want to meet or see you, either.

- 🏠 Medium and large dogs generally need fenced-in yards and more exercise than smaller breeds.

- 🏠 Large dogs can live in apartments, provided they get ample walks and exercise throughout the day.

- 🏠 Large dogs are good for people who live athletic lifestyles or for those who need athletic dogs.

- 🏠 Medium-size dogs often offer a compromise between large and small dogs.

There are caveats to these rules. Older, calmer dogs can work well in a low-activity household, especially if they're couch potatoes. On the other hand, Terrier crossbreed dogs can be very active (Jack Russell Terrier crossbreeds, for example) and would not necessarily be suited to a home that requires a dog with a low activity level.

Should You Get Two?

If you have a dog already, choosing a designer dog who is the opposite sex and about the same size will help prevent squabbles. (Although dogs will sometimes get aggressive with the opposite sex, it's less likely.)

But what about getting two puppies? Unless you've raised a puppy before, you're in for a handful. One puppy is a lot of work; two puppies are exponential harder.

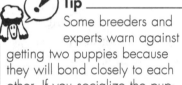

Tip

Some breeders and experts warn against getting two puppies because they will bond closely to each other. If you socialize the puppies properly, the puppies will bond to you as well.

Will a Designer Dog Be an Outside Dog?

Designer dog were bred primarily for human companionship, and they need to be inside with their humans. If you can't keep him inside with you, perhaps you should reconsider owning a designer dog.

What If You Have Children?

Many designer crossbreeds come from breeds that are normally very good with gentle and conscientious children; however, some dogs simply won't get along with kids and some kids shouldn't have dogs.

If you have children, you need to consider them before getting a dog. Every year, children are bit—some seriously—because their parents left them alone with a dog or they don't understand the difference between a dog and a stuffed toy. Dogs aren't playthings, and even the gentlest dog might bite if he's in pain or provoked. If you have very young children, you must teach them that dogs are not toys and can feel pain. And never leave a young child unsupervised with a dog at any time.

Toy and small dogs are especially at risk around children. Because they're so small, a young child can inadvertently hurt a dog without meaning to, and the little dog can bite and cause serious injury as well.

Warning _____
Don't buy a puppy "for the kids." A dog needs a responsible adult to care for him.

Older children can help you care for the dog, but the care should always be under adult supervision.

Where to Get Your Designer Dog

Purchase your designer dog from a reputable breeder (see Chapter 4) or adopt from a shelter or local rescue group (see Chapter 5). These are the only places you should look for a dog, not only because health and temperament will be more consistent, but also to not support those breeders with questionable practices.

You're going to pay a lot of money for your designer dog, so shouldn't you buy the very best dog you can for your money? Prices for dogs from reputable breeders are often no more than from pet stores, puppy mills, and backyard breeders. When you buy from a reputable breeder, you're buying quality.

Where *Not* to Get Your Designer Dog

Sadly, the most obvious places for people to buy a dog are often the worst places to buy from. This includes commercial breeders, puppy mills, and pet stores.

Backyard Breeders

The backyard breeder might be your neighbor, a friend, or someone not far from you who decides that breeding dogs might be a good idea and hopes to sell the puppies to good homes. Some backyard breeders are well intentioned, but many are only in it for the money. After all, they've seen the prices of many designer dogs.

Most backyard breeders are first-time breeders or otherwise very inexperienced at breeding. In many cases, their dogs don't come from quality stock, they haven't done all the necessary genetic screening, nor do they understand that they have to do this to produce a quality dog. For example, you might see a backyard breeder boasting "hips checked." This usually means he or she asked the vet once if the hips looked all right but didn't get any certifications done.

Will you get a good pet if purchased from a backyard breeder? Hard to say. Some have produced decent pets, but many dogs with inherited diseases are also turned out. Backyard breeders inevitably contribute to the pet-overpopulation problem by producing substandard dogs, and will neither guarantee their health, nor take back the dog if there's a problem.

> **Warning**
> Hip dysplasia and other hereditary joint problems can cost thousands of dollars in surgery and medications to fix—assuming they can be remedied. Some problems are so severe that euthanasia is the only humane thing you can do.

Another type of backyard breeder isn't necessarily inexperienced but have bred their dogs quite often. On first blush, they look like they might be a reputable breeder. They're too small to be considered a true commercial breeder, but often they breed for money, not for temperament or any sort of health standard.

Puppy Mills

Also called "puppy farms," puppy mills are commercial breeders who breed litter after litter and sell puppies for the sole reason of making a profit. Puppy mills usually have dozens or even hundreds of dogs and produce several litters a year.

Very few puppy mills do the necessary tests to produce healthy dogs with sound temperaments. Dogs are usually kept in rows of kennels or cages, and the worst puppy mills keep dogs in substandard conditions: filthy cages without adequate water and food. Often the female is bred at every season or heat so she can continue to produce puppies without a rest until she is too old or worn out. Puppies are taken from their mothers too early and shipped to pet stores. Puppies are seldom socialized—there are too many dogs for the commercial breeder to care for.

Puppy mills produce dogs not to offer a quality pet, but rather, to offer a pet for a price. If you have the money, chances are, a puppy mill breeder will sell you a puppy no matter what your lifestyle or circumstance is. You might get a healthy dog, but in many cases you won't. Some puppy mills offer health guarantees but may caveat them with unreasonable conditions. Even if you do get a guarantee, it's little comfort when you've grown attached to a dog who has a serious health problem.

Just as there are well-meaning backyard breeders, there are probably well-intentioned puppy mill breeders as well. However, their dogs are unlikely to be a quality product because of the sheer number of dogs produced, lack of socialization, and lack of genetic screening.

Pet Stores

You might be surprised to see pet stores on the list of where not to buy a dog. Pet stores usually get their puppies from commercial breeders and occasionally from backyard breeders, but never from reputable breeders, because reputable breeders screen their buyers. It is impossible for a breeder to effectively screen a buyer who purchases a puppy from a pet store.

Some pet stores have started carrying adoptable dogs and cats from local shelters. This is the only time it's acceptable to get a dog from a pet store.

The Least You Need to Know

- Only buy your designer dog from a reputable breeder, or adopt your dog from a shelter or rescue.

- Your choice of a designer dog depends on your lifestyle and family.

- Do not buy a designer dog from a puppy mill, backyard breeder, or a pet store.

Chapter 4

Buying a Designer Dog from a Breeder

In This Chapter

- 🏠 Finding and choosing a breeder
- 🏠 Learning what genetic testing and health certifications your potential puppy should have
- 🏠 Understanding the contracts and other paperwork that come with your new designer dog
- 🏠 Buying an out-of-town dog and shipping home your designer puppy

You've decided to look for a designer dog, and you now know that if you're going to buy a puppy, you should buy from a reputable breeder. But how do you find one? Look in newspapers? Do a web search?

In this chapter, I give you guidelines for finding and choosing a breeder, then help you understand all the paperwork that comes with your designer dog. And after you've picked your dog, you'll need to get him home. This chapter helps with that, too.

Finding a Reputable Breeder

Because designer dogs are popular and yet not a standardized breed, it's sometimes hard to determine whom you should buy your dog from. Where do you start your search?

Locating a Breeder

With crossbreeds, you usually don't have a parent organization such as the American Kennel Club (AKC) to get a breeder referral from. Some popular crossbreeds such as the Labradoodle have a national breed club that might have listings of breeders in their organization. That's a good place to start, certainly (see Appendix B for listings).

> **Did You Know?** _____
>
> Many health-registry databases are available free online. You can find out if the parents of your potential pooch really have been certified to be free of certain hereditary diseases such as hip dysplasia, eye diseases, or von Willebrand's disease (a blood-clotting disorder). Go to Appendix B for a listing of health registries and their websites.

But what if there's no club? You might have to do a little legwork on your own. Here are some tips to help your search:

🏠 Contact veterinarians, dog trainers, and dog groomers in your area and explain that you're looking for a particular crossbreed. Ask if they know of anyone who owns (or breeds) such a dog and if they might be willing to talk with you.

🏠 If the dog is bred for competition, such as Border Collie and Jack Russell Terrier crosses, a local agility or flyball club might point you in the right direction.

🏠 Ask someone who already owns a dog of the breed you're thinking of. Ask where he got his dog and if he would recommend the breeder. If the person is happy with his dog, he'll be happy to share the information.

🏠 Try the Internet and local newspapers. But because many puppy mills take out ads online and in papers, this should be your last resort, not your first choice. Reputable breeders do advertise here, too, but most of the time, you'll find puppy mills before you find the legitimate, responsible breeder.

Warning _____

Don't embrace everyone who is nice to you who wants to sell you a puppy. The people who run puppy mills are often very nice people because they *want* you to buy their dogs—and they want your $2,500. If someone was going to pay you $2,500, you'd probably be nice to that person, too.

Qualifying Your Breeder's Reputation

Don't rely on what breed clubs or other people tell you when it comes to determining whether a breeder is reputable or responsible. Only you can make that determination by asking questions—tough questions—that disreputable breeders will act offended by.

No breeder can fully guarantee the genetic health and long life of the puppy you're about to purchase, but he can offer proof that the parents were screened for inherited diseases and provide some sort of guarantee that the puppy is free of certain hereditary defects and diseases. (More about this later in the chapter.)

Tip _____

Most breeders should be able to provide references of clients who were happy with their dogs, too. Call these references and ask them about their experience with the breeder and their dog.

As you talk to your dog's potential breeder, look and listen for a few warning signs of a disreputable breeder:

🏠 "Puppies always available."

🏠 "We don't need to screen hips (eyes, elbows, or whatever) because crossbreeds (Labradoodles, Cockapoos, Peekapoos, etc.) don't have these problems."

🏠 "Crossbreeds are healthier."

🏠 "Hypoallergenic dogs."

🏠 "They're going fast—if you don't buy now, they'll be gone."

🏠 "Kid-friendly."

Warning
Looking for a designer dog among responsible dog owners and breeders might make you feel like you're baiting piranha. The dog world is heavily divided on the issue of whether these dogs should even exist, and you're going to get a lot of flak when you ask questions, so expect it. When someone tries to talk you out of getting a designer dog, thank the person for the advice and move on. You have a dog to look for!

When checking to see if a breeder is reputable, keep these points in mind:

🏠 The breeder produces no more than three litters a year. Puppies are *not* always available.

🏠 The breeder has been breeding these crossbreeds for several years.

🏠 If there is a club (local or national), the breeder is a member.

🏠 The breeder is able to provide documented proof that the puppies' parents were screened for inherited diseases (OFA, CERF, etc.; see the "Health Certifications" section later in this chapter for more).

🏠 The breeder will offer a guarantee to replace the puppy or refund your money if the puppy is sick or has an inherited disease the breeder screens for.

🏠 The breeder will require you to spay or neuter your puppy if he is to be a pet.

🏠 The breeder will agree to take back the dog under *any* circumstance.

🏠 The breeder will have a contract that spells out the guarantees regarding the health of the dog.

🏠 The breeder breeds no more than two breeds.

🏠 The breeder will not try to convince you to buy a puppy right now.

🏠 The breeder waits until the female dog is 2 years old before breeding.

Did You Know?

Why is the age of the mother dog important? Most dogs (including crossbreeds) don't fully mature physically and emotionally until they reach 2 years old, and the Orthopedic Foundation for Animals (OFA) doesn't certify hip x-rays for dogs younger than 24 months. Dogs start their estrus (heat cycle) around 6 months of age, but breeding a dog that young is equivalent to a 12-year-old human girl having a baby. Any dog younger than 2 is still growing and still maturing.

🏠 The breeder only breeds a female once a year so she can recover from an earlier breeding.

🏠 The breeder is looking for a specific type and temperament in his or her dogs.

🏠 The breeder takes an interest in the people buying her puppies. She will ask about your lifestyle and family situation to determine whether you're a good candidate for her dogs.

- The breeder is able to give you referrals.

- If the crossbreed is bred as a performance dog, the breeder should participate in the activity.

- The breeder does not allow a puppy younger than 8 weeks to leave her kennel.

- The breeder is available and willing to answer questions and remain accessible to you after you take home your new dog.

If you're having problems finding someone who meets the criteria for being a reputable breeder, keep looking. If you're spending money for a crossbreed dog that costs twice or more than a purebred, you should expect the same rigorous standards that reputable purebred breeders have. Otherwise, you risk purchasing a dog with problems.

Visiting the Breeder

You've qualified your breeder, and now you're ready to visit him or her in person. Remember, it's okay and even expected for you to ask lots of questions.

The dogs will either be in kennels or will be house pets. The kennels should be clean and well maintained, and the dogs should look healthy and nicely groomed and be friendly. Any puppies should be happy and curious, not crying or sickly.

Tip

Some breeders might not have puppies available when you visit. That's okay; visit the breeder anyway. It'll give you some time to get to know the breeder and decide if this is a person you'd like to buy your puppy from.

All dogs should be approachable. Be wary of any breeder who has an aggressive dog or one who the breeder tells you to stay away from. *Stud dog* or *bitch* should not be keywords for "mean dog." Do be careful around a female dog with her puppies, though. She is naturally protective of her puppies and might not appreciate your presence.

Nothing at the breeders, from the numbers of dogs and puppies present (which might suggest a puppy mill) to the condition of the dogs, to the dogs' temperament, should raise any warning flags.

When talking to the breeder, she should be able to tell you not only about the parents of your prospective puppy, but also about his grandparents, aunts, uncles, cousins, great-grandparents, etc. The breeder should be able to show you photo albums of the dogs in your puppy's background and what kind of dogs she produces. This is important if you want an idea of how your puppy will look and behave.

Checking Health Certifications and Contracts

If you're pleased with how everything looks while visiting the breeder, your next step is to request to look at health certifications. Be sure the certifications are original documents and not photocopies. The most widely known registration databases are the Orthopedic Foundation for Animals (OFA) and the Canine Eye Registry Foundation (CERF). (Other certifications include PennHIP, Optigen, and VetGen; see the "Health Certifications" section later in this chapter.) The original OFA document is printed with a blue background and has the words *Orthopedic Foundation for Animals, Inc.* The OFA seal should also be present. An original CERF certificate is printed white with blue background and has the word *Original* printed in red ink.

If the stud dog isn't owned by the breeder, photocopies of his health certificates are acceptable. Write down the dog's names so you can later look up the names in the OFA and CERF databases.

Warning
Disreputable breeders can be pretty unscrupulous. Some actually forge health certificates by photocopying the original certificate and then whiting out and typing in a different name so their dog is shown to have passed the certification. Ask to see the original certificates.

Also, ask the breeder for a copy of the contract. The breeder should give you a copy for later perusal if you're not buying a puppy right now.

What Do All These Documents Mean?

When you purchase your designer dog from a breeder, you shouldn't just get the dog and that's it. You should expect a certain amount of paperwork, too—contracts, registrations, and testing or health certifications. When sorting through all the documentation on your dog or potential dog with a breeder, it helps to know what all these documents mean.

Genetic Testing

The most common type of testing some breeders mention is "*genetic testing*," of which there are three types: parentage, disease screening, and coat color screening.

Definition _____

If a trait or disease is **genetic**, it is hereditary, or inherited through the genes.

Warning _____

Parentage genetic testing can be a valuable tool as long as the breeder is reputable. Breeders can still falsify documents, making a particular claim as to parentage that won't be disproven except through running your own genetic tests.

Parentage Testing

Parentage genetic testing important to determine or confirm the sire of the offspring. Some breed registries, such as AKC and United Kennel Club (UKC), allow DNA testing to prove parentage of a particular litter (this is useful on occasions where more than one dog may have bred the female or the sire is in question).

Note, this test doesn't check for certain colors or traits or even diseases. It only confirms that the puppies are progeny of certain dogs.

Disease Screening

Disease screenings look for certain genes that have been known to cause disease. Available through VetGen, Optigen, and other genetic testing facilities (see later in this chapter), these tests look for specific identified genetic components that cause known hereditary disease in certain breeds.

Unfortunately, these tests can't check for all diseases, nor do they test for many of the common diseases, such as hip dysplasia, which have several genetic and environmental components to them. Some of these tests look for rare genetic disorders that might not be applicable to your type of crossbreed.

These tests are also expensive and must be done one at a time. Ask the breeder of your potential puppy if she has had some of these tests done, and ask to see the certifications.

Coat Color Testing

The coat color test is only available for certain purebreds. It won't tell you how many puppies will be born with a certain coat color, but it will give you the possible color combinations, given the parents' genetics.

Health Certifications

Some diseases are so widespread in dogs that they affect almost all breeds and mixed breeds in some capacity. Hereditary joint problems affect nearly every breed, including small dogs (the highest number of dysplastic dogs include Bulldogs and Pugs).

These diseases are often caused by the same genes across all breeds, and when those genes in one breed get paired with the same genes in another breed, the result is an unhealthy crossbreed. This is why health certifications are so important.

Unfortunately, there isn't just one simple test to screen out all the nasty genes. However, you can determine if the parents of the puppies in question are clear of the disease. The thought is that if the parents, grandparents, great-grandparents, etc., are clear of the disease, the puppies are less likely to have the disease. Although this is not fool-proof (recessive genes can still lurk, unexpressed, in a gene pool), testing and breeding only those dogs who are clear of the disease reduces the chances of passing on problems. Some dog breeds prone to certain inherited diseases actually have *improved* because of this testing and registration with databases such as OFA, CERF, PennHIP, Optigen, VetGen, and others.

Orthopedic Foundation for Animals (OFA)

OFA was developed for screening out diseases such as hip and elbow dysplasia. OFA has added additional screening for other diseases, including the following:

- **Hip dysplasia,** a malformation of the hips; seen in all breeds and crossbreeds.

- **Elbow dysplasia,** a malformation of the elbow joint; seen in all breeds and crossbreeds.

- **Cardiac problems,** seen in all breeds and crossbreeds.

- **Patellar luxation**, a genetic kneecap slippage due to anatomical deformities; seen primarily in small and medium-size dogs.

- **Legg-Calve-Perthes disease,** a genetic hip-joint disease; seen primarily in small and toy dogs.

- **Hypothyroidism and hyperthyroidism**, which might be genetic; seen in all breeds and crossbreeds.

- **Congenital deafness,** acquired or inherited.

- **Sebaceous adenitis,** a hereditary inflammation of the sebaceous glands in the skin, causing allergylike symptoms; seen primarily in Poodles, Akitas, and Samoyeds and their mixes.

Tip
Because OFA has a variety of rankings depending on the disease, check out the meanings at www.offa.org.

OFA gives a variety of possible results for each of these tests. For example, in hip dysplasia, a dog might rank *excellent, good, fair, borderline,* or *dysplastic* (with *mild, moderate,* or *severe* ranking), while a dog who is tested for Sebaceous Adenitis may rank *no evidence (at the time of the evaluation), affected, affected without clinical symptoms,* or *equivocal.*

> **Warning**
>
> Although some breeds and crossbreeds are less likely to have certain diseases, any breed or crossbreed can have almost any inherited disease. Don't accept the breeder's word. When a breeder says the dog has "had hips checked," it could mean anything from the breeder looking at the dog's hips, to his asking the vet if he thinks the dog is okay, to an actual certification. Ask for proof of certification, and write down the parents' names. You can then check to see if the dog(s) are indeed in the OFA database.

Canine Eye Registry Foundation (CERF)

CERF provides a database for dogs with eye problems. The parents must be examined by a veterinary ophthalmologist, who will give the dog a *pass* or *fail* rating. This examination is good for one year.

University of Pennsylvania Hip Improvement Program (PennHIP)

PennHIP is another certification for hip dysplasia. Like the OFA certification, PennHIP uses x-rays to determine the extent of hip dysplasia and to certify whether or not the dog has the disease.

VetGen

VetGen, a genetic research facility, offers tests for the following diseases:

- **Von Willebrand's disease (vWD),** a type of hemophilia present in several breeds.
- **Renal dysplasia (RD),** an often deadly hereditary kidney disease that affects certain breeds.

🏠 **Copper toxicosis (CT),** a hereditary disease in which copper accumulates in the liver, causing a fatal liver disease.

VetGen also offers coat color tests for certain purebreds.

Optigen

Optigen offers testing for progressive retinal atrophy for a number of breeds. Progressive retinal atrophy is a hereditary eye disease that leads to blindness.

The Contract

Ask the breeder if he or she has a *contract*. The contract is your bill of sale and protects you if something goes wrong with your dog such as a health problem, or if you can't keep him or no longer want him. A truly reputable breeder will take back the dog no matter what the circumstance and no matter how long it's been since you purchased the dog.

> **Definition**
> The **contract** is the bill of sale between you and the breeder. It holds legal obligations such as right of first refusal, spay/neuter clauses, and health guarantees. It is a piece of paper that protects you and gives you legal recourse should anything go wrong either with your purchase or with your dog's health. If the breeder does not have a contract, look elsewhere.

In the contract, the breeder should also guarantee his or her puppy to be free from illnesses, parasites, and hereditary defects. (No one can full guarantee their dogs completely free, but they should offer a guarantee to refund or replace the puppy should there be a problem.) Again, most of these guarantees have reasonable time limits. Breeders usually require that the owner take the puppy to the vet within the first week to ensure the puppy's health.

Most breeders will replace or refund the dog at the breeder's discretion—small consolation if your designer dog has hip dysplasia and you're already attached to him. Be sure to do your legwork and verify that the breeder has screened for diseases.

If the breeder has a limited clause on a refund, don't expect to get your money back after a year. You also might not get a refund on behavioral problems that arise or on health issues not guaranteed in the contract.

Warning

Be careful: many breeders have a "Right of First Refusal" or "First Right of Refusal" in their contract. This means the breeder has the *option* of taking back the dog, and he is not required to. Some breeders use this clause as a way of *looking* responsible without following through.

A reputable breeder will stipulate in the contract that you must adequately care for the puppy and require that you never allow your puppy to run at large. The contract should not have stud rights or requirements for breeding unless this is something you've agreed with prior to seeing the contract. The guarantee should not have a caveat requiring such things as strange diets or extreme limitation of exercise.

Most likely your designer dog will be sold as a pet, and the breeder should have a spay/neuter clause in the contract, which requires you to spay or neuter your pet at the appropriate time (before 6 months of age), or when you purchase the dog if the breeder hasn't spayed or neutered the dog already. (This indicates a responsible breeder who will not contribute to animal overpopulation.)

Depending on the breeder, you might see other stipulations in the contract. If you don't understand something in the contract, have a lawyer look over it.

Registration Papers—or Not

Certain designer dogs such as the Labradoodles and Cockapoos have their own breed club and registry (see Appendix B), but you can't register a designer dog with the AKC. If the breeder is a member of a national or international club, request registration papers.

If you want to compete in performance competitions with your designer dog, you can register with the UKC to compete in obedience, agility, and other performance events.

Health Records

The breeder should also furnish your prospective puppy's health records. Note these are not the same as health certificates. These records include vaccinations, dewormings, and any other health-care history pertinent to your prospective puppy's health.

Buying from an Out-of-Town Breeder

Sometimes the nearest breeder of your designer dog is in another state. It's always best that you meet with the seller face to face, and most reputable breeders want to meet their puppies' buyers. After all, reputable breeders don't sell to unknown buyers.

Warning

Unless you visit the breeder, you're relying on the breeder's integrity to ship you a healthy puppy who will fit in well with your family and situation. Some truly unscrupulous people can pose as breeders, and once you send the money, they disappear without a trace.

If you're determined to buy a dog from a seller you've never met, do as much screening as you can on the Internet and over the phone. Ask the same questions you would to a breeder in your area to weed out the potential puppy mills and backyard breeders, and use the Internet to verify health certificates.

Ask for references, and after contacting those references, see if the reference will recommend that you speak to someone else. Using an Internet search engine such as Google on the breeder's name or kennel name might yield more information (both good and bad) about the breeder.

If the breeder checks out, consider flying or driving to check out the breeder. You'll be spending extra on a plane ticket or gasoline, but consider it part of the cost of owning a designer dog.

Buying from an Overseas Breeder

If you're buying from an overseas breeder, you'll have to be sure the seller is indeed very reputable or you may find yourself out of a lot of money—not only the cost of the dog but also the shipping costs (see the next section). Talking with the breeder and talking with references will help a lot, but there are no guarantees here and very little recourse if you've been scammed.

You'll also have to think about customs. Check with U.S. customs regarding the current laws for bringing pets into the United States. You might have to pay a tariff depending on what country your dog is shipped from.

It will also take time to ship your dog. Be prepared to wait for your dog to arrive (use this time to puppy-proof your home or send out new puppy announcements).

Shipping Your Designer Dog

If you buy your designer dog from across the country or from another country, be sure you have a way of shipping the puppy to you. Shipping a dog is very difficult. Keep these things in mind when shipping a dog:

- If you're going to fly to get the dog, notify the airline when making your travel arrangements that you'll be bringing a dog with you, and get as much information in advance concerning what you need to do to ship a dog.

- Regulations are constantly changing when it comes to shipping pets. Contact the airlines for current rules and paperwork.

- Some smaller airplanes can't accommodate more than one pet on board, so be sure there's enough space available.

- Most airlines won't ship a pet during very hot or very cold seasons for the safety of the animal. Although most, if not all, major airlines have pressurized and climate-controlled baggage compartments—where your dog will be held—temperatures can vary and your dog can be subject to very cold or very hot temperatures. Be mindful of the temperatures outside, and plan accordingly.

- Choose a direct flight or one with no flight changes.

Tip

Pet-shipping services are available for weaving through the red tape when it comes to airlines and shipping pets. Contact the Independent Pet and Animal Transportation Association International at www.ipata.com. (*Note:* this is for informational purposes only; neither the author nor the publisher endorses this company.)

- Contact the airline to find out the cost of shipping a pet. Most charge by the weight, but many charge by the dog's size as well. The cost of shipping a dog varies, but you're likely to pay $200 or more for a one-way ticket for your pet. Add to that the cost of an airline-approved travel kennel, health certificates, tariffs, and any customs costs (if applicable), and you're likely to pay $500 or more to ship your new pet home.

- You'll need to purchase an airline-approved travel kennel with bowls for food and water. You (or the breeder) will have to provide enough food for the flight in case there's a delay or if the flight is longer than 8 hours.

🏠 It's a good idea to have your dog microchipped before he travels, in case he gets lost (see Chapter 15). Microchipping might make things easier when traveling from other countries as well, as it is a permanent way of identifying and tracking your dog.

🏠 Before shipping your puppy, you'll have to have a health certificate from a veterinarian who has examined your puppy within 8 days of his flight. A copy of the health certificate needs to stay taped onto the animal's crate, and you should carry the original with you if you're flying with him.

Warning

I've shipped dogs by plane with no problems, but I've heard stories of people (and dogs) who weren't as lucky. While the airlines do everything they can to ensure a safe flight for our furry friends, accidents do happen.

🏠 Depending on how old your puppy is, he needs to be current on his vaccinations before shipping. These vaccinations should be listed on his health certificate.

Tip

Check out some of these helpful websites for shipping and traveling with pets:

🏠 U.S. Department of Transportation: tinyurl.com/456er

🏠 USDA Guidelines to import pets: www.aphis.usda.gov/NCIE/pet-info.html

🏠 International Air Transport Association Traveler's Pets Corner: www.iata.org/whatwedo/live_animals/pets

The Least You Need to Know

🏠 Only buy your designer dog from a reputable breeder.

🏠 Be certain the breeder has a contract. The contract is your bill of sale. If there's anything in the contract you don't understand, consult a lawyer.

🏠 Understand and ask for documentation of health screenings and certification before you purchase your dog.

🏠 Be sure your contract has a clause that will require the breeder to take back the dog in any case within the contract. Look for health guarantees within the contract as well.

🏠 Shipping your designer dog home can be expensive and time-consuming. Be sure you have up-to-date shipping info and regulations before you ship your dog.

Adopting a Designer Dog

In This Chapter

- 🏠 Finding happiness at a shelter or rescue program
- 🏠 Locating a shelter or rescue group with designer dogs
- 🏠 Visiting shelters and rescue groups: what to look for
- 🏠 Expanding your search: finding your designer dog online

You've decided a shelter dog or a dog from a rescue group will work well with you and your family. Maybe you want a designer dog but realize buying a puppy from a reputable breeder is too pricey for your budget. Or maybe you know all about the pet overpopulation and would rather have a slightly "used" designer dog from a shelter or rescue group.

Regardless of your reasons, good for you! You can find happiness—and a perfect pet—with a shelter or rescue dog while saving a life and also helping to alleviate further pet overpopulation.

Choosing a Dog from a Shelter or Rescue Group

Approximately 5 million pets fill local shelters and rescue groups annually—including many designer dogs who didn't quite fit for whatever reason. Shelters are usually teeming with mixed breeds and crossbreeds—three quarters of all dogs at a shelter, to be exact.

Owners give up their dogs for a variety of reasons: they didn't have time for a dog, or their child had allergies and the dog wasn't hypoallergenic, or the dog couldn't be trained for whatever reason, or maybe the owners just remodeled the house and the dog didn't fit with the décor. Whatever the reason, if the dog is in a shelter that puts down the animals it cannot adopt out within a specified time period (often called a *kill shelter*), that dog has a good chance of being killed, especially if he is older than a few years (puppies tend to find homes more quickly).

 Tip
Most rescue groups and shelters have older puppies and dogs rather than 8-week-old puppies. The older pups might not be at the "oh so adorable" stage anymore, but they're still pretty cute and will bond to you just as well as an 8 week old.

 Definition
A **kill shelter** puts down dogs after a certain amount of time or when the shelter becomes full.

When you adopt a dog from a shelter or rescue group, you save a life and don't contribute to the growing pet overpopulation problem. And you save money, too, usually: if you can find him, you can get a designer dog at a shelter or from a rescue group without the designer price. Most adoption fees are somewhere between $50 and $300.

But there are negatives, too, the biggest being is that quite often you don't know the dog's history. The dog might have an unseen medical condition that could show up later. Or the dog could have learned bad habits from his previous owners who didn't take the time to properly train him. And if you're set on breeding your dog, maybe a shelter isn't the way to go, as most shelters require you spay or neuter your adopted dog.

Did You Know? _____

Don't rule out an older puppy or dog. Even dogs who haven't had a lot of attention as puppies can still bond closely with people if the person is willing to take the time to work with the dog.

Finding a Shelter or Rescue Group

Most shelters list themselves in the Yellow Pages under "animal shelters." Many rescue groups advertise in the newspaper. Some list themselves with veterinarians and trainers. Others might list themselves at the local shelter. You might have luck with a local Internet search as well. Just type "animal shelter" and your city in your favorite search engine.

Visiting the Shelter

When you're looking for a designer dog in a shelter, it pays to call ahead or go online and find out if they have the type of dog you're looking for and, more important, if he's still there. When you've determined that the dog you're interested in is still there, you might have to look around a bit to find him or ask a staff member. If you go alone, be sure the shelter has a hold policy; that is, if you decide on a dog, they will hold him for you until your family members can meet him. Sometimes it's better to "scout out" a new pet alone before taking your family with you. But regardless, you should have your family involved in the final decision-making process.

Be aware that the shelter is a very stressful place for animals, and your prospective dog is unlikely to behave normally in such a high-stress environment. If you can, meet with the dog one on one (see the following "Meeting One-on-One" section), but keep in mind that a one-on-one meeting in the shelter might not tell you much.

A better strategy is to talk with the shelter staff about your prospective dog. They can usually tell you why the dog was surrendered to the shelter, how old he is, and what kind of crossbreed he is (see the following "Is the Dog a Designer Breed?" section). They can also tell you about his temperament and help you determine if he's the right dog for you.

Adopting the Dog from a Rescue Group

Adopting a dog from a rescue group is a lot like adopting a dog from the shelter, with one important difference: dogs in rescue are typically at foster homes and are usually more relaxed and well socialized with the foster family. Depending on how long they've had him, the foster family can usually tell you about the dog, and they should be honest with you how the dog behaves and what bad habits he might have. The foster family might know the dog's background better than a shelter worker would, too.

Meeting One on One

Whether you've found a shelter or rescue dog, meeting the dog one on one is very important even if it doesn't give you the entire picture. Meet the dog in a quiet room if you can. See how he reacts to you. Is he cringing and fearful or friendly and outgoing? It's okay for the dog to show some trepidation followed by cheerful acceptance. If he continues to act fearful or submissive—or act wild and unruly—you probably don't want this dog. You want the dog to act friendly.

Warning

For safety's sake, never adopt a dog with a known aggression problem, no matter how sorry you feel for him. Plenty of other well-adjusted dogs are waiting for homes.

Next, put the dog on a leash and walk him. See how he reacts to you and to the leash. If he knows any commands, work with him and see how he reacts. If you see any aggression or questionable behavior, you might want to find another dog. (See Chapter 6 for more on choosing your perfect pooch.)

Is the Dog a Designer Breed?

How can you tell if the dog you're considering is a designer dog or a mutt? You can't—not by looks alone, anyway. Designer dogs are crossbreeds, and a lot of mixed breeds in shelters are just that—crossbreeds. You have to look at the dog and guess—or ask the shelter staff or breed rescue. Most shelters and rescue groups have some clue what breeds their dogs are because either the owner told them or they can make a few educated guesses.

You'll usually find three types of crossbreeds in the shelter:

- Crossbreed dogs who are "accidents." Quite often, purebred owners don't spay or neuter their pets because they feel that their dog is very valuable. However, 63 days after the one time their dog gets out of the yard, they have puppies!

- Crossbreed dogs whose owners may have turned them over to a rescue group or to a shelter. These dogs might or might not be from reputable breeders—sometimes owners are embarrassed to admit they couldn't keep the dog or the paperwork has been lost.

- Crossbreed dogs from backyard breeders who thought they could make money by producing a designer dog.

When You Can't Find a Designer Dog Locally

If you've been to your local shelter and can't find a designer dog or no rescue groups nearby handle these dogs, look regionally and perhaps nationwide. There can be pitfalls associated with this you should be aware of, though.

Rescue and Shelter Restrictions

Some shelters and rescue groups will not adopt dogs outside a certain state or region. This is for the dog's sake, because the shelter or rescue group doesn't want someone taking a dog to a region where they can't check up on him.

Many shelters and rescue groups will not adopt a dog to people who do not have fenced-in backyards or to people who live in apartments. Many won't consider placing even a small or toy dog with someone who does not have a fenced-in backyard.

Good shelters and rescue groups will grill you about whether you'll be a good pet owner and ask such questions as these:

- Have you ever owned a dog before? What happened to that dog?

- Why are you interested in getting a dog?

- Do you plan on having the dog spayed/neutered?

- Do you have a fenced-in backyard?

- Who will be the dog's primary caretaker?

- How many people are in your family? Who will interact with the dog?

- Do you have other pets?

- Do you have children?

- For how long are you away from home each day?

- Will this be an indoor or an outdoor dog?

Expect the interrogation, and don't be put off. Shelters and rescue groups want to be sure their dogs are going to good homes.

Choices and Limitations of Adoption

When you're looking for a dog to adopt, you might run into snags, depending on how choosy you are. For example, although young puppies are available, most shelters and rescue groups have older puppies, adolescents, and adult dogs. You're unlikely to find an 8-week-old puppy (though occasionally you do see them).

You also might have difficulty finding the exact crossbreed you want. For example, you might want a mini Labradoodle, but all you can find at your local shelter and rescue group today are a Cockapoo and a Goldendoodle. You might not have a choice of age, sex, or color.

And if you're looking for an intact dog, you might have to look somewhere else. Most shelters and rescue groups require that you spay or neuter your dog after adoption. This shouldn't be an issue, though, if you're getting a pet.

> **Tip**
> Some shelters and rescues are put off by people looking for a "designer" pet and don't believe that anyone looking for such a pet would be a good adopter. When you're looking for a crossbreed, ask the shelter or rescue for the mix, not the cutesy name: ask for a Poodle and Labrador mix, not a Labradoodle. Some shelters and rescue might be okay with the name Labradoodles; some won't be.

Finding an Adoptable Pet Online

The Internet is a great resource when you're looking for a pet. Many shelters, including local shelters, now have websites where you can search for just the right dog. Be careful, though! Many shelters don't update their websites nearly enough, and a dog who was on a list might not be available when you go to the shelter to see him. Likewise, new dogs who just were brought in might not be listed when you search.

Several nationwide services help match people and pets. Usually these services are linked to local shelters but may not include listings for all shelters. Some good websites to look for pets include the following:

- **Pet Finder (www.petfinder.com).** Search locally, regionally, or nationally.

- **Pets 911 (www.1888pets911.org).** Another great adoption site.

- **Best Friends (www.bestfriends.org).** A no-kill shelter that adopts pets.

- **Adopt-a-Pet (www.adoptapet.com).** Offers a list of shelters throughout the country.

- **Rescue Poodle-Mix Dogs (www.fpv.com/rescuedogs.html).** An adoption place for Poodle mixes.

- **Doodle Rescue and Rehomes Board (disc.server.com/Indices/213827.html).** Another adoption place for poodle mixes.

Regardless of where you find your dog, you still need to visit the dog to be sure this is the right pet for you.

The Least You Need to Know

- Animal shelters and rescue groups are good places to find the perfect designer dog for you.

- You can't tell visually if a dog is a designer crossbreed or just a mutt. Talk to shelter or rescue staff to get some more information.

- Whether at a shelter or a rescue group, choose a dog who is friendly and outgoing and responds well to you and your family.

- You can even search online to find a potential pet.

Chapter 6

Choosing Your Perfect Puppy or Dog

In This Chapter

🏠 Choosing the best puppy or adult dog for you

🏠 Basing your selection of a puppy or adult dog on more than just looks

🏠 Determining your potential dog's temperament and personality

You've found the right breeder or perhaps the right dog from a rescue group or a shelter, but as cute as puppies and even adults are, looks are only skin deep. How do you ensure that your new designer dog is healthy and happy and has the right temperament?

Selecting Your Puppy

Puppy selection often depends on the breeder. Some will select the puppy for you; others will let you chose from the litter. Don't be put off if the breeder selects the puppy or makes recommendations for which puppy might suit you best. She's spent a tremendous amount of time evaluating puppies and has been with the litter you're considering since they were born. She looks at the puppies with an eye for which puppy might fit you best, considering you, your family, your interests, and your lifestyle. You'll probably find she's a good match-maker.

If the breeder doesn't select a puppy for you, you might still want to ask her opinion. Ask her about the puppies' personalities and which ones might be right for you. In most cases, you'll want a puppy who is neither too dominant nor too submissive.

Tip

For your dog's safety in the car, bring a crate with you when you go to chose or pick up your designer puppy or dog. Don't have someone hold the dog in his lap; the dog could squirm away and cause you to have a traffic accident.

Looks Aren't Everything

If the breeder lets you pick your own puppy, be careful. Most people choose a pet for all the wrong reasons, and looks tops that list. Just because you like the dog's color or the way a puppy looks doesn't mean the relationship will work. Like people, some puppies and dogs aren't going to mesh with your personality.

Choosing a Healthy Puppy

Of course you want a healthy puppy. Healthy puppies are everything you expect them to be: active, healthy-looking, bright-eyed, and full of energy. Sick puppies will cry, appear listless, have poor hair-coats, runny noses, potbellies, and goopy eyes. Healthy puppies might be inactive when they first wake up, but they should start moving around once they wake.

You'll want to check the puppy's eyesight and hearing. Roll a ball or wave a toy in front of his face to see if he will react. Clap your hands or snap your fingers behind his head to see if he will turn his head and look or at least react. These tests aren't scientific, but they might show if there is an eyesight or hearing problem.

Always bring your puppy for a full examination by a veterinarian within 72 hours of purchase.

Temperament Testing

When you visit the puppies, call to them. They should come to you readily. The first puppy who greets you might be more dominant, but this largely depends on where the puppies were when you called them. Puppies who visit and then wander off might be independent-minded. These free spirits could be difficult to train because they're more interested in their surroundings than in you. Likewise, puppies who hang back or act fearful might be too submissive.

Active is good, but hyper isn't. Let the puppies calm down a bit and play with them. Puppies who play very aggressively with their siblings or with you might be too dominant.

At this point, with the breeder's approval, separate each of the puppies you're considering from their siblings and play with them. Most puppies might become a little nervous when they're separated from their litter, but as you're playing with them, they'll usually become cheerful and relaxed. If the puppy you're thinking of buying becomes fearful, aggressive, or overly hyper, look at another puppy.

With the breeder's permission, gently pick up the puppy and cradle him so he's on his back. Some puppies with become very fearful or will struggle violently when held or turned up. A calm and self-assured puppy will perhaps struggle a little and then relax as you give him a tummy rub. If the puppy reacts very negatively—either fearfully or aggressively—set him down.

You want a puppy who will react positively to the experience of meeting you. He can be a little fearful at first, but he should then follow with cheerful acceptance.

Selecting Your Adult Dog

Selecting an adult dog is a little easier. Unlike puppies, the adult dog is basically "what you see is what you get," unless it is an older puppy. If you can find out the adult dog's history or talk to the owner, do so.

If the dog has been a breeder return, ask the breeder why the dog was returned to her. If the dog is at a shelter or with a rescue, sometimes the staff will be able to tell you why the dog is there. Be aware that previous owners often will lie about why the dog is being returned. A typical response is "allergies," so don't always believe that the former owner returned your prospective dog or dumped him in the shelter because someone suddenly became allergic to him.

Warning

No matter how sorry you feel for the dog or how much you like him, never choose a dog who bites people or who has an aggression problem. He is a liability. Plenty of well-adjusted dogs are available for purchase or adoption.

People typically relinquish their pets because of behavioral problems (many of which are easily corrected by someone willing to take the time to train them); inconvenience (the owner didn't have time); a lifestyle change; or the owner moved away, died, or couldn't afford the dog anymore.

Looks Aren't Everything

As with puppies, you need to choose a dog beyond good looks. When you take a dog into your house, you're making a commitment to him to give him a good home. Unfortunately, someone has already reneged on that promise and the dog now needs a good home, so be certain of your choice.

Choosing a Healthy Adult Dog

As much as you might feel sorry for dogs with special needs, think about what it will cost to fix the problem—assuming you can fix it at all. Cancer, heartworm, serious injuries, and congenital or hereditary defects can all be very costly—sometimes upward of several thousands of dollars. Unless you know what you're getting into, don't choose one of these dogs.

Ask to see the dog's health records, if any are available. Dewormings, vaccinations, and heartworm preventive should be up to date. Look at the dog, too. He should appear healthy, with no obvious symptoms or illnesses. His eyes should be bright, his breath fresh, his mucous membranes discharge-free, and he should be healthy and happy.

 Warning

Dogs who have serious medical conditions are best left to those with the resources or knowledge to handle them.

The final check should be done by a veterinarian, of course, within 72 hours of purchase.

Temperament Testing

Temperament testing with an adult dog is much harder to do, because you certainly don't want to roll a dog on his back! (That's a sign of dominance, and even a well-adjusted dog is most likely to fight back and bite!) Instead, approach a dog as a complete unknown.

Let the dog meet you, preferably alone in a quiet room without distractions. See if he's interested in you or whether he doesn't seem to care if you're there or not. If he's not interested, or interested in something else, it might be a sign that he's very independent.

He might be a little wary at first, and that's okay, but once you allow him to sniff your hand, he should be friendly and accepting. When meeting strangers, some dogs are a bit hyper, so wait and see if he calms down.

His expression should be soft and gentle; he shouldn't be staring at you angrily or cringing while you talk to him or hold out your hand. Many dogs won't meet your gaze, so that's okay—it's a sign of submissiveness. Consider looking elsewhere if you notice any aggression or extreme shyness.

The dog should respond well to your voice and to petting. If the breeder, owner, or shelter allows you to offer the dog a treat, do so. Does he take the cookie gently, or do you have to count your fingers afterward? Although taking a cookie quickly might be expected, growling or showing aggression over food is definitely not a good thing and is something you'll have to work on if you get this dog. It doesn't have to be a black mark against getting this dog, though.

Did You Know?

It takes a while for a dog to settle into his new family and new surroundings. You might not see the dog's true personality for days or even weeks.

Tip

Always have a contract and some way to return an adult dog if he doesn't work out.

Next, if the dog knows commands, try some. If you can, take him for a walk on a leash and see how he does with that. Is he pulling hard, or does he walk nicely? If he pulls, you'll have to work on this if you get him.

Don't ignore anything that raises a red flag with you. The dog might be perfectly fine, but he might not be fine *for you*. Trust your instincts if this doesn't seem to be the right fit.

Otherwise, if the dog seems to do well with you, you may have found a good pet.

The Least You Need to Know

- Select a puppy, who is neither too submissive nor too dominant.

- Choose an adult dog who is friendly and outgoing and responds well to you.

- Never rely solely on looks when choosing a puppy or dog.

Part  Bred by Design: A List of Designer Dogs

You've decided that a designer dog is in your future, but which designer dog is right for you? What kind of dog are you looking for? Are you looking for a "Poo" dog, a performance dog, or maybe a specialized crossbreed?

In Part 2, I cover the most popular crossbreeds—and also a few you might not have heard about. You can compare and contrast these dogs and decide for yourself which designer is the one for you.

(Photo courtesy of Earl A. Gershenow)

Chapter 7

The "Poo" Dogs

In This Chapter

- Meeting the various Poo dogs: the Labradoodle, the Cockapoo, and others
- Comparing and contrasting the Poo crossbreeds
- Looking for a Poo breeder

In this chapter, you meet the "Poo" crossbreeds—those crossbreeds that are part Poodle. These dogs often have an open coat, which might make them more tolerable to people with allergies.

Because of the newness of some of the crossbreeds, the Poo dogs aren't always easy to find. But when you do find them, you're in for a treat.

Labradoodles (Labrador Retrievers + Poodles)

(Photo courtesy of Lori Herrold)

(Photo courtesy of Ken Fischer)

(Photo courtesy of Lori Herrold)

"What kind of dog *is* that?" is the typical question a Labradoodle owner hears. Because they're such friendly and outgoing dogs, most people who meet Labradoodles fall in love with them quickly and become ardent supporters of the crossbreed. Labradoodles come in three sizes—miniature, medium, and standard—and single-coat Labradoodles might be good pets for those with allergies.

Breed Characteristics

Origin: Australia, 1989

Coat: Fleecy single coat, woolly curly coat, or Labradorlike coat (short, medium, or long); medium to low shedding

Low allergy: Yes

Colors: Apricot, gold, red, black, buff, brown (chocolate), cream, red, silver, and chalk

Grooming needed: High; needs regular clipping and daily brushing and combing

Trainability: Moderate to high

Sizes: Varies: *Miniature:* 12 to 16 inches; *Medium:* 17 to 20 inches; *Standard:* 21 to 24 inches or more

Activity level: Medium to high

Good with other pets: Usually

Good with children: Yes, but needs supervision

Health problems: Progressive retinal atrophy, patella luxation, hip dysplasia, elbow dysplasia, and hypothyroidism

Life span: 10 to 15 years

Registry: International Labradoodle Association

First generation or generational: Both

Breed History

Labradoodles were first bred to be guide dogs in Australia in 1989 by Wally Conran (or Cochran). The idea was to breed assistance dogs who did not shed and were hypoallergenic. The popularity of the Labradoodle has grown considerably since that time.

Meet the Labradoodle

The Labradoodle is a smart and active dog with an outgoing personality, who is suitable for being a companion. Labradoodles combine some of the best features of the Poodle and the Labrador: intelligence, outgoing personality, and a need to be with people.

Many but not all Labradoodles have single coats, and some do shed. Some breeders have a good idea if their lines will produce single or double coats, but there's still a chance that genetics will throw in a double coat here or there.

The Labradoodle's personality is largely dependent on the personalities of the parents and other ancestors, but most breeders say Labradoodles have great temperaments and are good with children. Discrepancies do exist, however, especially in dogs of mixed breeding, and any dog could bite if provoked. Therefore, it's very important that you screen for a dog or puppy with a good temperament and never leave small children alone with any dog, even one as amiable as the Labradoodle.

> **Tip**
>
> Many people look for "doodle dogs" because they suffer from allergies but still want a dog. Be certain you can tolerate a doodle dog before you buy one and then discover you can't!

Labradoodles come in a number of different colors, ranging from black to white and anything in between. And first-generation Labradoodles might favor either the Labrador Retriever or the Poodle side, depending on the mix. Generational dogs tend to blend into the more standard Labradoodle look.

Labradoodles can be a mix of Miniature through Standard Poodle with any Labrador Retriever, hence the three sizes.

Should you decide that the Labradoodle is right for you, look for a breeder who breeds for temperament; screens for patella luxation, hip dysplasia, and elbow dysplasia; and screens for eye problems.

Warning

Be careful of breeders who warn that high-protein diets or too much exercise cause hip dysplasia or elbow dysplasia. Both of these conditions are caused by a complex interaction of *genetics* and possibly in some cases, extreme environmental conditions. There's no such thing as dysplasia that is solely environmentally induced. If you feed your dog a diet approved by the Association of American Feed Control Officials (AAFCO) and he doesn't run in a sled team or jump higher-than-hock height in agility, there's absolutely no way you can cause dysplasia in your dog.

Where to Find a Labradoodle

Contact the International Labradoodle Association (www.ilainc.com) for a list of breeders.

Goldendoodles (Golden Retrievers + Poodles)

(*Photo courtesy of Earl A. Gershenow*)

(*Photo courtesy of Earl A. Gershenow*)

With the success of the Labradoodle, the next logical step is the Goldendoodle, or a cross between a Golden Retriever and a Poodle. This is a relatively new crossbreed, having appeared within the past few years.

Did You Know?

Most designer dogs aren't standardized and don't have "breed clubs" associated with them. Sometimes you'll have to find a breeder either through word of mouth or by doing an Internet search. Regardless of how you find a breeder, hold that breeder to the same standards as all other reputable breeders. You're paying a lot of money for this dog, and you deserve the very best.

Breed Characteristics

Origin: United States, early 2000s

Coat: Fleecy single coat, woolly curly coat, or Goldenlike coat (short, medium, or long); medium to low shedding

Low allergy: Yes

Color: Gold

Grooming needed: High; needs regular clipping and daily brushing and combing

Trainability: Moderate to high

Size: *Standard:* 21 to 24 inches or more

Activity level: Medium to high

Good with other pets: Usually

Good with children: Yes, but needs supervision

Health problems: Progressive retinal atrophy, patella luxation, hip dysplasia, elbow dysplasia, allergies, and hypothyroidism

Life span: 10 to 15 years

Registry: None

First generation or generational: First

Breed History

The Goldendoodle is a relatively new crossbreed developed by many breeders who bred Labradoodles and decided to try a new crossbreed.

Meet the Goldendoodle

The Goldendoodle, like the Labradoodle, is a smart and active dog with an outgoing personality, who is suitable for being a companion. Goldendoodles combine some of the best features of the Poodle and the Golden Retriever: intelligence, an outgoing personality, and a need to be with people.

Many but not all Goldendoodles have single coats, and some do shed. Because they are in their first generation, there are bound to be some dogs with undercoats and those who do shed.

The Goldendoodle's personality is largely dependent on the personalities of the parents and other ancestors, but most breeders say Goldendoodles have great temperaments and are good with children. Discrepancies exist, however, especially in dogs of mixed breeding, and any dog could bite if provoked. Therefore, it's very important that you screen for a dog or puppy with a good temperament and never leave small children alone with any dog, even one as amiable as the Goldendoodle.

Goldendoodles are primarily golden in color. They might eventually show colors found in Poodles. Depending on the genetics, the Goldendoodle may resemble either parent.

Currently, there is only a standard size for Goldendoodles. That might change if the crossbreed becomes popular.

Allergies are common in both Poodles and Golden Retrievers, so be sure there is no history of allergies in either parent. These will often show up as skin problems.

Warning _____

Registration of the parent dogs with clubs such as American Kennel Club (AKC) or United Kennel Club (UKC) is *not* a guarantee of quality. Be certain the breeder also does health certifications.

Should you decide that the Goldendoodle is right for you, look for a breeder who breeds for temperament; screens for patella luxation, hip dysplasia, and elbow dysplasia through OFA or PennHIP; and screens for eye problems through either CERF or Optigen.

Where to Find a Goldendoodle

At the time of this writing, no club promoting the Goldendoodle exists, so your best bet is to ask trainers and veterinarians and perhaps search on the Internet. Some Labradoodle breeders breed Goldendoodles, too, so check with those breeders.

Cockapoos (Cocker Spaniels + Poodles)

(Photo courtesy of Debbie Cowdrey)

(Photo courtesy of Debbie Cowdrey)

(Photo courtesy of LTYCOL Mary D. Foley, United States [Ret])

You've probably seen or heard of Cockapoos, those Cocker Spaniel and Poodle crossbreeds. They've been around a long time and have won many people's hearts. Cockapoos come in a variety of sizes and colors to suit almost anyone looking for a fun dog. Their single coat reduces shedding and dander, making them a candidate for people with allergies.

Breed Characteristics

Origin: United States, 1950s

Coat: Open with wavy texture; low to no shedding

Low allergy: Yes

Colors: Apricot, black, buff, chocolate, cream, red, silver, and white

Grooming needed: High; needs regular clipping and daily brushing and combing

Trainability: Moderate to high

Sizes: Varies: *Teacup toy:* 4 pounds and less, shorter than 10 inches at the shoulder; *Toy:* under 10 pounds, about 10 inches at the shoulder; *Mini:* 10 to 20 pounds, 10 to 14 inches at the shoulder; *Standard:* 20 to 30 pounds, 14 to 17 inches at the shoulder; *Giant:* 30 pounds and more, 17 inches and higher at the shoulder

Activity level: Low to medium

Good with other pets: Usually

Good with children: Yes, but needs supervision

Health problems: Progressive retinal atrophy, various eye problems, allergies, patella luxation, hip dysplasia, and Legg-Calve-Perthes disease

Life span: 10 to 15 years

Registry: North American Cockapoo Registry; Cockapoo Club of America

First generation or generational: Both

Breed History

The Cockapoo is a crossbreed that's been around since the 1950s. Most likely, an accidental breeding occurred and the breeders found that the resulting dogs made wonderful pets. Since that time, various breeders have bred Cockapoos, some claiming this was a new breed and charging a fair amount of money for the dogs.

Meet the Cockapoo

Most Cockapoo owners point out that their dogs are friendly, outgoing pets who combine the best of the Poodle and Cocker Spaniel. Their wavy coat isn't quite like a Poodle's, but they have no undercoat and, therefore, shed less and might be better tolerated by people with allergies.

Did You Know?
You'll hear a lot of breeders talk about F1 and F2 stock. *F1* is simply a term for "first generation." *F2* is a generational dog who has been bred from two F1s.

Warning
Be cautious of any breeder who registers his dogs with "nonstandard" breed clubs—those other than the AKC or UKC. Some simply exist to legitimize puppy mill stock but have no real guidelines as to what makes a breed.

The Cockapoo's personality is largely dependent on the personalities of the parents and other ancestors, but most Cockapoos are touted as having great temperaments and are good with children. Discrepancies do exist, however, especially in dogs of mixed breeding, and any dog could bite if provoked. Therefore, it's very important that you screen for a dog or puppy with a good temperament and never leave small children alone with any dog, even one as amiable as the Cockapoo.

Cockapoos can be any color that comes from either the Poodle or Cocker Spaniel. And first-generation Cockapoos might resemble either the Cocker Spaniel or the Poodle side, depending on the mix. Generational dogs tend more to blend into the standard Cockapoo look.

Because Cockapoos can be a mix of any Poodle (Toy through Standard) with any Cocker Spaniel, there's a size discrepancy among the breed. Cockapoos can be less than 4 pounds or more than 50 pounds, depending on the dog.

Should you decide that the Cockapoo is right for you, look for a breeder who breeds for temperament; screens for patella luxation, hip dysplasia, Legg-Calve-Perthes disease through OFA; and screens for eye problems through CERF or Optigen.

Where to Find a Cockapoo

Check the breeder referral with the North American Cockapoo Registry (NACR; www.cockapoos.com) or the Cockapoo Club of America (www.cockapooclub.com) for potential breeders. You could also talk to veterinarians, groomers, and trainers.

Peekapoos (or Pekapoos) (Pekingese + Poodles)

The Peekapoo is a fairly old crossbreed similar to the Cockapoo, and in fact, many breeders of Peekapoos tend to breed other small crosses as well. The Poodle genes in the Peekapoo tend to improve the health problems normally seen in brachycephalic dogs such as the Pekingese.

Breed Characteristics

Origin: United States, 1950s

Coat: Open with wavy texture; low to medium shedding

Low allergy: Yes

Colors: Apricot, black, buff, chocolate, cream, red, silver, and white

Grooming needed: High; needs regular clipping and daily brushing and combing

Trainability: Moderate

Size: Varies: 4 to 20 pounds

Activity level: Low to medium

Good with other pets: Usually

Good with children: Yes, but needs supervision

Health problems: Progressive retinal atrophy, patella luxation, hip dysplasia, Legg-Calve-Perthes disease

Life span: 10 to 15 years

Registry: None

First generation or generational: First

Breed History

Peekapoos were either accidental crosses of a Pekingese and a Poodle or they were purposely bred by people who had luck with Cockapoos and decided to try their hand with another crossbreed.

Meet the Peekapoo

Peekapoos are usually smaller than Cockapoos and might have the temperaments of both the Pekingese and the Poodle. Their wavy coat isn't quite like a Poodle's, but they have no undercoat and, therefore, shed less and might be better tolerated by people with allergies.

Peekapoos might have great temperaments or be reserved, depending on the mix and the personalities of the parents and other ancestors. They're small and might not be good with small children, who can antagonize them because of their size. Any dog could bite if provoked. Therefore, it's very important that you screen for a dog or puppy with a good temperament and never leave small children alone with any dog.

Peekapoos can be any color that comes from the Poodle or Pekingese. Because there's no standard, there can be quite a size difference among these dogs.

Should you decide that the Peekapoo is right for you, look for a breeder who breeds for temperament; screens for patella luxation, hip dysplasia, and Legg-Calve-Perthes disease through OFA; and screens for eye problems through either CERF or Optigen.

> **Warning**
> When looking for a dog who does well with children, you must first ask yourself if your child is ready for a small dog. No matter how careful a young child is, he or she could easily but unintentionally hurt a small or toy dog. If you have small children, consider a bigger dog.

Where to Find a Peekapoo

Currently no club for Peekapoo breeders exists, so your best bet is to look for a breeder of Cockapoos or other Poo dogs. Ask veterinarians, trainers, etc., or look on the Internet.

Schnoodles (Schnauzers + Poodles)

(Photo by Renee Pierce, Pierce Schnoodles)

(Photo by Renee Pierce, Pierce Schnoodles)

The Schnoodle (or Snoodle) is a crossbreed between a Miniature Schnauzer and Miniature Poodle; sometimes Standard Schnauzers or Toy Poodle are mixed, too. Some breeders decided that the single coat of both breeds would make a delightful pet for those with allergies, and the size would be ideal for people looking for a smaller dog.

Breed Characteristics

Origin: United States

Coat: Open with wavy texture; low to medium shedding

Low allergy: Yes

Colors: Gray, black, apricot, black and tan, buff, chocolate, cream, red, silver, white, and sable; usually a mix of colors

Grooming needed: High; needs regular clipping and daily brushing and combing

Trainability: Moderate

Size: Varies: 10 to 20 pounds, 12 to 15 inches or more depending on the size of the parents

Activity level: Medium

Good with other pets: Usually

Good with children: Yes, but needs supervision

Health problems: Eye problems, patella luxation, hip dysplasia, and Legg-Calve-Perthes disease

Life span: 10 to 15 years

Registry: None

First generation or generational: First

Breed History

The Schnoodle is most likely an experimental cross developed because of interest in the Poo crossbreeds.

Meet the Schnoodle

Schnoodles are crosses between Schnauzers and Poodles, usually between the smaller varieties of each breed. Schnoodles are typically cute—adorable to many—like most of the Poo dogs. Their coat is somewhere between a Poodle's curls and a Schnauzer's hard, wiry hair. Both breeds have no undercoat and therefore shed less. People with allergies might better tolerate these dogs.

The Schnoodle's personality is largely dependent on the personalities of the parents and other ancestors, but many Schnoodle owners and breeders say they have great temperaments and are good with children. Discrepancies do exist, however, especially in dogs of mixed breeding, and any dog could bite if provoked. Therefore, it's very important that you screen for a dog or puppy with a good temperament and never leave small children alone with any dog.

Schnoodles can be any color that comes from the Poodle or Schnauzer and are often two colors.

Size-wise, the Schnoodle depends on the size of the parents. A Giant Schnauzer and a Standard Poodle will produce a much bigger dog than will a Miniature Schnauzer and a Toy Poodle.

Should you decide that the Schnoodle is right for you, look for a breeder who breeds for temperament; screens for patella

Warning

Not all crossbreeds are good breeds. In fact, in some crossbreeds, crossbreeding can actually cause worse problems because genes combine in unlikely ways. This is why it's very important to have dogs screened for inherited problems.

luxation, hip dysplasia, and Legg-Calve-Perthes disease through OFA; and screens for eye problems through CERF and Optigen.

Where to Find a Schnoodle

A club for Schnoodle breeders doesn't yet exist, so your best bet is to look for a breeder of Cockapoos or other Poo dogs. Ask veterinarians, trainers, etc., or look on the Internet.

Yorkipoos (Yorkshire Terriers + Poodles)

(Photo courtesy of Bonnie Wagenbach)

(Photo courtesy of Bonnie Wagenbach)

The Yorkipoo is a cross between a Poodle and a Yorkshire Terrier—two cute dogs who produce an even cuter crossbreed.

Breed Characteristics

Origin: United States

Coat: Open with wavy texture; medium to low shedding

Low allergy: Yes

Colors: Gray, black, apricot, black and tan, buff, chocolate, cream, red, silver, white, and sable; usually a mix of colors

Grooming needed: High; needs regular clipping and daily brushing and combing

Trainability: Moderate

Size: Varies: 4 to 17 pounds, 7 to 15 inches or more depending on the size of the parents

Activity level: Medium

Good with other pets: Usually

Good with children: Yes, but needs supervision

Health problems: Eye problems, patella luxation, hip dysplasia, Legg-Calve-Perthes disease, and liver shunts

Life span: 10 to 15 years

Registry: None

First generation or generational: First

Breed History

The Yorkipoo is most likely an experimental cross developed because of interest in the Poo crossbreeds.

Meet the Yorkipoo

A cross between Yorkshire Terriers and Poodles, the Yorkipoo's coat might be more like a Poodle's or a Yorkie's (or somewhere in between). They have no undercoat and, therefore, shed less and might be better tolerated by people with allergies.

Yorkipoos might have great temperaments, or they might be reserved, depending on the mix and the personalities of the parents and other ancestors. They're small and might not be good with small children, who can antagonize them because of their size. Any dog might bite if provoked. Therefore, it's very important that you screen for a dog or puppy with a good temperament and never leave small children alone with any dog.

Yorkipoos can be any color that comes from Poodles or Yorkies. Because there's no standard, there can be quite a size difference among these dogs.

Should you decide that the Yorkipoo is right for you, look for a breeder who breeds for temperament; screens for patella luxation, hip dysplasia, and Legg-Calve-Perthes disease through OFA; and screens for eye problems through either CERF or Optigen. Yorkies are prone to liver shunts, which can be fatal and might be passed genetically to Yorkipoos.

> **Tip**
>
> To understand what potential health problems exist within a crossbreed, do your research, look at both breeds, and see which dogs might have the same or similar problems. Although some genes that carry diseases are recessive, many are dominant—and crossbreeding won't solve the problem.

Where to Find a Yorkipoo

No club for Yorkipoo breeders exists currently, so your best bet is to look for a breeder of Cockapoos or other Poo dogs. Ask veterinarians, trainers, etc., or look on the Internet.

Maltipoos (Maltese + Poodles)

(Photo courtesy of Shirley Kitelinger)

(Photo courtesy of Shirley Kitelinger)

Maltipoos, many of which are 4 pounds and very tiny, are possibly the cutest of the designer breeds. They're a cross between Maltese and Toy or Miniature Poodles.

Breed Characteristics

Origin: United States

Coat: Open with wavy texture; medium to low shedding

Low allergy: Yes

Colors: Gray, black, apricot, black and tan, buff, chocolate, cream, red, silver, white, and sable

Grooming needed: High; needs regular clipping and daily brushing and combing

Trainability: Moderate

Size: Varies: 4 to 17 pounds, 7 to 15 inches or more depending on the size of the parents

Activity level: Medium

Good with other pets: Usually

Good with children: Yes, but needs supervision

Health problems: Eye problems, patella luxation, hip dysplasia, and Legg-Calve-Perthes disease

Life span: 10 to 15 years

Registry: None

First generation or generational: First

Breed History

The Maltipoo is most likely an experimental cross developed because of interest in the Poo crossbreeds.

Meet the Maltipoo

Maltipoos are a cross between Maltese and Toy or Miniature Poodles. Their coat might be more like a Poodle's or a Maltese's, or somewhere in between. They have no undercoat and, therefore, shed less and might be better tolerated by people with allergies.

The Maltipoo personality is largely dependent on the personalities of the parents and other ancestors, but most have great temperaments—but they can be spoiled rotten if not properly trained. They're small and might not be good with small children, who can antagonize them because of their size. Any dog may bite if provoked. Therefore, it's very important that you screen for a dog or puppy with a good temperament and never leave small children alone with any dog.

Maltipoos can be any color that comes from the Poodle or white. Because there's no standard, there can be a size difference among these dogs.

Did You Know?

Often, many of these crossbreeds were accidental breedings and someone came up with a cute name. You can find some of the same types of dogs at shelters—for a lot less money!

Should you decide that the Maltipoo is right for you, look for a breeder who breeds for temperament; screens for patella luxation, hip dysplasia, and Legg-Calve-Perthes disease through OFA; and screens for eye problems through either CERF or Optigen.

Where to Find a Maltipoo

There's no club for Maltipoo breeders yet, so your best bet is to look for a breeder of other Poo dogs. Ask veterinarians, trainers, etc., or look on the Internet.

Other Poo Dogs

As you might expect, the crosses between Poodles and other breeds know few bounds. Designer dog breeders look to breed a number of different dogs to provide a dog who has a single coat (and, thus, is more allergy friendly) and may have a different look. If you're interested in a Poo dog, check out the following:

🐾 **Shihpoos (or Pooshihs) (Shih Tzus + Poodles).** The mix is intended to reduce the brachycephalic head of the Shih Tzu while still providing an adorable dog with a single coat.

🐾 **Poochons (Poodles + Bichons Frises).** This cross introduces another variety to the Poo dogs, providing a very gregarious dog.

(Photo courtesy of Bonnie Wagenbach)

(Photo courtesy of Bonnie Wagenbach)

🐾 **Bassadoodles (Basset Hounds + Poodles).** This cross might reduce the long-backed problems of the Basset and might provide a single wavy coat of the Poodle.

🐾 **Sheltipoos (Shetland Sheepdogs + Poodles).** This mix provides the intelligence of the Sheltie and the Poodle and might produce a single coat.

The Least You Need to Know

- Most Poo crossbreeds provide variations and are good dogs for people looking for a companion.

- Many Poo crossbreeds don't have breed clubs, which means you often have to do some searching, either on the Internet or by asking around to find a breeder.

- Many of the smaller Poo breeds aren't suitable for very young children, who can accidentally hurt them.

Performance Designer Dogs

In This Chapter

- 🏠 Meeting the dogs bred for agility, flyball, and sled dog racing
- 🏠 Understanding why performance dogs don't necessarily make good pets for everyone
- 🏠 Learning the history of the performance dogs

Whether it's pulling a sled, leaping over flyball hurdles, or climbing over an A-frame in agility, performance dogs are the top of their league when it comes to competition. In this chapter we'll look at some of the performance crossbreeds and what they're best at.

Border Collie Terriers (Border Collies + Jack Russell Terriers)

(Photo courtesy of Jean Fogel)

In the quest for the perfect flyball or agility dog, some breeders have taken two of the top performing dogs, Border Collies and Parson Russell Terriers (PRT) or Jack Russell Terrier (JRT), and put them together for a fast, smart speed demon on the agility and flyball courses. Sometimes called the Border Terrier (not to be confused with the AKC Border Terrier), these Border Collie Terriers combine the size of the Parson Russell Terrier and the agility of both breeds.

Breed Characteristics

Origin: United States, 1990s

Coat: Double coat; short to medium; sheds

Low allergy: No

Colors: Black and white

Grooming needed: Medium; needs weekly brushing and combing, especially during seasonal shedding

Trainability: High

Size: Varies: 12 to 22 inches at the shoulder, 15 to 45 pounds

Activity level: High

Good with other pets: Maybe

Good with children: No

Health problems: Hypothyroidism, epilepsy, hip dysplasia, and eye problems

Life span: 10 to 15 years

Registry: None

First generation or generational: First

Breed History

These dogs were developed for competition in the 1990s.

Meet the Border Collie Terrier

The Border Collie Terrier is a crossbreed built for performance sports. Those who compete in the sports of agility and flyball have long looked for a dog who can perform best on lower jump heights.

All Border Collie Terriers have double coats. They can shed quite a bit, but that's not what they're bred to do. Depending on which genes they inherit, they can be either like the Border Collie or the JRT, or a bit like both in temperament or looks.

They're usually black and white, but they can be any color in either breed.

The Border Collie Terrier inherits his personality from both parents, so it's important that the parents have good temperaments. Some Border Collies and JRTs can be snappish and standoffish and will pass along those traits to their offspring. Some may be friendly. They are usually not good with children.

These dogs are generally high energy and make lousy house pets if they have nothing to do. Older, retired dogs usually make fine pets, but puppies and young adults tend to have more energy and usually aren't suitable as pets.

Should you decide that the Border Collie Terrier is right for you, look for a breeder whose lines are friendly and whose dogs will enjoy human companionship. If you buy puppies, look for someone who screens for hip dysplasia, elbow dysplasia, and hypothyroidism and who screens for eye problems.

Where to Find a Border Collie Terrier

Check with agility organizations and flyball organizations that allow mixed breed dogs, such as the United States Dog Agility Association (USDAA; www.usdaa.com), North American Dog Agility Council (NADAC; www. nadac.com), and North American Flyball Association (NAFA; www.flyball.org). Rescue groups and shelters frequently have these dogs as well because their high energy level makes them too much for many people to handle.

Border Shepherds (Border Collies + Australian Shepherds)

(Mai Idzkowski and the Nike Animal Rescue Foundation; narfrescue.org)

(Mai Idzkowski and the Nike Animal Rescue Foundation; narfrescue.org)

As with the Border Collie Terrier, some breeders have tried to create the perfect flyball or agility dog by taking two of the top performing dogs, Border Collies and Australian Shepherds, and putting them together for a fast, smart speed demon on the agility and flyball courses. The Border Shepherd combines the agility and trainability of both breeds.

Breed Characteristics

Origin: United States, 1990s

Coat: Double coat; short to medium; sheds

Low allergy: No

Colors: Black and white, blue merle (dark blue against lighter gray background), red merle, and tricolor; any color that exists in the parent breeds

Grooming needed: Medium; needs weekly brushing and combing, especially during seasonal shedding

Trainability: High

Size: Varies: 15 to 22 inches at the shoulder, 35 to 55 pounds

Activity level: High

Good with other pets: Maybe

Good with children: No

Health problems: Hypothyroidism, epilepsy, hip dysplasia, eye problems, and deafness

Life span: 10 to 15 years

Registry: None

First generation or generational: First

Breed History

These dogs were developed for competition in the 1990s.

Meet the Border Shepherd

The Border Shepherd is a crossbreed built for performance sports. These dogs do well in agility, flyball, and herding.

All Border Shepherds have double coats. They can shed quite a bit, but that's not what they're bred to do. Depending on which genes they inherit, they can be either like the Border Collie or the Australian Shepherd, or a bit like both in temperament or appearance.

They can be any color in either breed.

The Border Shepherd inherits his personality from both parents, so it's important that the parents have good temperaments. Some Border Collies and Australian Shepherds can be snappish and standoffish and will pass along those traits to their offspring. Some may be friendly. They are usually not good with children.

These dogs are generally high energy and make lousy house pets if they have nothing to do. Older, retired dogs usually make fine pets, but puppies and young adults tend to have more energy and usually aren't suitable as pets.

Should you decide that the Border Shepherd is right for you, look for a breeder whose lines are friendly and whose dogs will enjoy human companionship. If you buy puppies, look for someone who screens for hip dysplasia, elbow dysplasia, and hypothyroidism, and who screens for eye problems. There might or might not be breeders, so consider a rescue group or a shelter as another option.

Where to Find a Border Shepherd

Check with agility organizations and flyball organizations that allow mixed breed dogs, including USDAA, NADAC, and NAFA. Rescue groups and shelters frequently have these dogs because their high energy level makes them too much for many people to handle.

Border Retrievers (Border Collies + Labrador Retrievers)

(Photo by Hilary Lane, courtesy of Rocky Mountain Border Collie Rescue)

(Photo by Hilary Lane, courtesy of Rocky Mountain Border Collie Rescue)

As with the Border Shepherd, some breeders have tried to create the perfect flyball or agility dog by taking two of the top performing dogs, Border Collies and Labrador Retrievers, and putting them together for a fast, smart speed demon on the agility and flyball courses. The Border Retriever combines the agility and trainability of both breeds, as well as the outstanding characteristics of the Labrador Retriever.

Breed Characteristics

Origin: United States, 1990s

Coat: Double coat; short to medium; sheds

Low allergy: No

Colors: Black and white, chocolate, yellow, and black; any color that exists in the parent breeds

Grooming needed: Medium; needs weekly brushing and combing, especially during seasonal shedding

Trainability: High

Size: Varies: 15 to 25 inches at the shoulder, 35 to 70 pounds

Activity level: High

Good with other pets: Maybe

Good with children: Maybe

Health problems: Hypothyroidism, epilepsy, hip dysplasia, eye problems, elbow dysplasia, and heart problems

Life span: 10 to 13 years

Registry: None

First generation or generational: First

Breed History

These dogs were developed for competition in the 1990s.

Meet the Border Retriever

The Border Retriever, like the Border Shepherd, is a crossbreed built for performance sports. These dogs do well in agility, flyball, and herding.

All Border Retrievers have double coats. They can shed quite a bit. Depending on which genes they inherit, they can be either like the Border Collie or the Labrador Retriever, or a bit like both in temperament or appearance.

They can be any color in either breed.

The Border Retriever inherits his personality from both parents, so it's important that the parents have good temperaments. The Labrador personality might outweigh the occasionally skittish

Border Collie personality and might make a good pet for someone with kids, but like any dog, it needs proper socialization and should never be left alone alone with children.

These dogs are generally high energy and make poor house pets if they have nothing to do. Older, retired dogs usually make fine pets, but puppies and young adults tend to have more energy and usually aren't suitable for pets.

Should you decide that the Border Retriever is right for you, look for a breeder whose lines are friendly and whose dogs will enjoy human companionship. If you buy puppies, look for someone who screens for hip dysplasia, elbow dysplasia, and hypothyroidism, and who screens for eye problems. They might or might not be breeders, so consider a rescue group or a shelter as another option.

Where to Find a Border Retriever

Check with agility organizations and flyball organizations that allow mixed breed dogs, including USDAA, NADAC, and NAFA. Rescue groups and shelters frequently have these dogs because their high energy level makes them too much for many people to handle.

Alaskan Huskies (Siberian Huskies + Alaskan Malamutes + Lurchers)

(Photo courtesy of Margaret H. Bonham)

(Photo courtesy of Margaret H. Bonham)

The Alaskan Husky is a specialized mixed/crossbreed bred especially for speed and endurance in sled dog races. These dogs have been around a long time, but in recent years, these dogs have been crossed with Siberian Husky, Pointers, and various sighthounds for speed.

Breed Characteristics

Origin: United States, 1900s

Coat: Double coat; short or medium preferred; sheds twice yearly

Low allergy: No

Colors: All

Grooming needed: Medium; needs weekly brushing and combing, especially during seasonal shedding

Trainability: Low to medium

Size: Varies: 20 to 27 inches at the shoulder, 35 to 85 pounds

Activity level: High

Good with other pets: No

Good with children: No

Health problems: Hypothyroidism, epilepsy, hip dysplasia, eye problems, and zinc-responsive dermatosis

Life span: 10 to 17 years

Registry: None

First generation or generational: Generational

Breed History

The Alaskan Husky has been around since the days of the Klondike when mushers (sled dog drivers) hooked up dogs to their sleds to pull them across the frozen wastelands. Originally, these dogs came out of Inuit villages and were mostly Husky, Malamute, or Village Dog. Later, as the Siberian Husky and other *Laika* (a type of Husky dog in Russia) breeds were imported from Russia, mushers looking for speed began to cross these dogs to make the bigger, faster sled dogs.

The result is the Alaskan Husky. Unlike true breeds, the Alaskan Husky is still a morphing crossbreed. Often mushers add Lurcher or other sighthound breeds to increase speed.

Meet the Alaskan Husky

The Alaskan Husky is the quintessential working dog. Bred for one purpose and one purpose only, he excels at sled dog racing, whether it's sprints, mid-distance, or long-distance racing.

All Alaskan Huskies have double coats. The coats are typically shorter than what people expect because the dogs tend to overheat with longer coats and exertion.

They can be any color, and depending on what they're being used for, they can have different builds as well.

Alaskan Huskies are bred for speed first and temperament second. They can be very friendly, or they may be shy and standoffish. Some dogs can be downright aloof. They are usually not good with children.

The energy level of the Alaskan Husky can best be described as hyper or frenetic. Some, usually older, retired dogs, can make good house pets, but puppies and young adults tend to have more energy and usually aren't suitable as pets.

Should you decide that the Alaskan Husky is right for you, look for a breeder whose lines are friendly and whose dogs will enjoy human companionship. If you buy puppies, look for someone who screens for hip dysplasia, and who screens for eye problems.

Where to Find an Alaskan Husky

You can find Alaskan Huskies through sled dog kennels. Most list through www.sleddogcentral.com or www.workingdogweb. com.

> **Tip**
>
> Many mushers don't screen their dogs for genetic diseases because these dogs aren't intended to go to the general public. If you decide to purchase a dog from a sled dog kennel, ask for a written guarantee of health and an option to return the dog if you find anything wrong with him. Although this might not protect you fully, it does offer you some protection if you get a dog from a musher.

Scandinavian Hounds (Alaskan Huskies + German Shorthaired Pointers or English Shorthaired Pointers)

"That doesn't look like a Husky!" you'd say when you saw this dog, and you're right. They're Scandinavian Hounds, a specialized cross-breed developed by Egil Ellis, an open sprint racer.

Breed Characteristics

Origin: United States, late 1990s

Coat: Double coat; short or medium preferred; sheds twice yearly

Low allergy?: No

Colors: All—usually dark or black

Grooming needed: Medium; needs weekly brushing and combing, especially during seasonal shedding

Trainability: Low to medium

Size: Varies: 20 to 27 inches at the shoulder, 40 to 55 pounds

Activity level: High

Good with other pets: No

Good with children: No

Health problems: Hypothyroidism, epilepsy, hip dysplasia, eye problems, and zinc-responsive dermatosis

Life span: 10 to 17 years

Registry: None

First generation or generational: Both

Breed History

Mushers have crossed German Shorthaired Pointers and English Shorthaired Pointers long before Egil Ellis, but his crossbreeds have made a comeback, and he has been the first to give them a name. Other mushers have tried to create these dogs as well, so you'll find plenty of German and English Shorthaired Pointer crossbreeds in mushing.

Meet the Scandinavian Hound

In the quest to build a better racing dog, one man, Egil Ellis, decided to rebreed German Shorthaired Pointers and English Shorthaired Pointers into Alaskan Husky stock to produce the Scandinavian Hound. Bred for one purpose and one purpose only, the Scandinavian Hound excels at sled dog racing, and particularly at sprint racing, although these dogs have made their way into mid-distance racing as well.

All Scandinavian Hounds have double coats. They're shorter than most Alaskan Husky coats.

They can be any color but tend to resemble the dark liver color of Pointers.

Scandinavian Hounds are bred for speed first and temperament second. They can be very friendly, or they may be shy and standoffish, but most are friendly. They are usually not good with children.

The energy level of the Scandinavian Hound is like the Alaskan Husky. Some, usually older, retired dogs, can make good house pets, but puppies and young adults tend to have more energy and usually aren't suitable as pets.

Should you decide that the Scandinavian Hound is right for you, look for a breeder whose lines are friendly and whose dogs will enjoy human companionship. If you buy puppies, look for someone who screens for hip dysplasia, and who screens for eye problems.

Tip

Two sledding organizations you might want to check out are the International Sled Dog Racing Association (ISDRA) at www. isdra.org and the International Federation of Sleddog Sports (IFSS) at www. sleddogsport.com.

Where to Find a Scandinavian Hound

Obviously, Egil Ellis has his true Scandinavian Hounds. Other mushers will have them as well. You can find Scandinavian Hounds through sled dog kennels. Most kennels list through www.sleddogcentral.com or www.workingdogweb.com.

The Least You Need to Know

- 🏠 Most of the performance crossbreeds are good dogs for people looking for a specialized performance dog in agility, flyball, or sledding.

- 🏠 Most performance crossbreeds don't have breed clubs, which means you often have to do some searching either on the Internet or by asking around to find a breeder. Sometimes contacting a performance organization will help you locate some breeders.

- 🏠 Most performance dogs aren't suitable for small children because they're active or they might not get along well with small children.

Chapter 9

Other Crosses

In This Chapter

- Checking out a few other crossbreeds
- Learning what to look for in other crosses
- Going behind the cute names of certain crossbreeds

In Chapters 7 and 9, you met a lot of popular and performance designer dog crossbreeds, and we're not done yet. In this chapter, you'll meet a few other crossbreeds. Many of these are one-offs and very difficult to find. Most are being bred by one or two breeders or may be the product of an accidental litter.

If you can't live without one of these dogs, look for a reputable breeder just as you would with a more popular crossbreed.

Dorgis (Dachshunds + Cardigan Welsh Corgis or Pembroke Welsh Corgis)

It sounds like a joke you might tell: "What do you get when you cross a Dachshund and a Corgi?" Answer: a Dorgi! With such a whimsical name, you can probably guess what results when you cross the feisty temperament of the Dachshund and the active Corgi.

Breed Characteristics

Origin: Great Britain, 2000s

Coat: Short coat; average shedding

Low allergy: No

Colors: Brown, brindle, golden, red, and black

Grooming needed: Medium to low; needs weekly brushing and combing; baths when necessary

Trainability: Moderate to high

Size: 10 to 15 inches, weight 20 to 40 pounds

Activity level: Medium to high

Good with other pets: Depends

Good with children: Good with older children

Health problems: Back problems, eye problems, and joint problems

Life span: 10 to 15 years

Registry: None

First generation or generational: First

Breed History

The Dorgi first developed due to a royal mishap: Britain's Princess Margaret's Dachshund, Pippin, accidentally bred with Queen Elizabeth II's Corgi. The resulting Dorgi litter was an instant success.

Meet the Dorgi

The Dorgi is a relatively new breed that has caught some designer dog enthusiasts' eyes, taking a Welsh Corgi (either the Pembroke or the Cardigan) and breeding it with the Dachshund. The result is a feisty combination with the energy and spunk of both breeds in a small package.

Putting together two long-backed dogs seems an odd choice, given that Dachshunds tend to suffer from an extraordinary amount of back problems, due mostly to structural reasons.

Dorgis can be any color that comes from the Corgi or the Dachshund lines.

Should you decide that the Dorgi is right for you, look for a breeder who breeds for temperament; screens for patella luxation, hip dysplasia, and Legg-Calve-Perthes disease; and screens for eye problems. Ask about back problems with their dogs.

Did You Know? _____

Although many toy breeds don't suffer from hip dysplasia as much as the larger breeds do, many smaller breeds suffer from Legg-Calve-Perthes disease, a condition in which the blood supply to the femoral head is interrupted and the bone cells die. The femoral head becomes deformed and causes a great deal of stiffness and pain.

Where to Find a Dorgi

Dorgis are still not very popular, and it might take some searching on the Internet or talking to veterinarians, groomers, and trainers to find one.

Bagels (Beagles + Basset Hounds)

(Photo courtesy of Diane Peters Mayer)

(Photo courtesy of Diane Peters Mayer)

No, I'm not talking about something to eat with cream cheese. A Bagel designer dog is a Beagle and Basset Hound cross. The Bagel looks something like a heavier-set Beagle or a taller Basset.

Breed Characteristics

Origin: United States

Coat: Short coat; average shedding

Low allergy: No

Colors: Tricolor

Grooming needed: Medium to low; needs weekly brushing and combing; baths when necessary

Trainability: Low to moderate

Size: 10 to 15 inches, weight 20 to 50 pounds

Activity level: Medium

Good with other pets: Usually

Good with children: Good with older children

Health problems: Back problems, eye problems, joint problems, epilepsy, von Willebrand's disease, and hypothyroidism

Life span: 10 to 15 years

Registry: None

First generation or generational: First

Breed History

A newer crossbreed, Bagels might have been an attempt at improving the Basset.

Meet the Bagel

The Bagel isn't necessarily a popular dog, but they seem to appear often enough to be worth mentioning. Sometimes specifically bred, but many times accidentally bred, the Bagel is an improvement on the problems associated with a long-backed dog.

Bagels are typically tricolor but can be any color from the Basset Hound or the Beagle lines.

Bagels typically have a Hound's personality; that is, independent and stubborn but also very loving.

Should you decide that the Bagel is right for you, look for a breeder who breeds for temperament; screens for patella luxation, hip dysplasia, and Legg-Calve-Perthes disease; and screens for eye problems. Ask about back problems and epilepsy with their dogs.

Warning

Be very careful when buying Beagle crossbreeds. Epilepsy is inherited in Beagles and might be passed along to crossbreeds. There currently is no genetic test for epilepsy.

Tip

Some of these crossbreeds aren't popular, so you may have to do quite a bit of looking to find them. It might be easier to go to a shelter or contact a small dog rescue group to find out if they have these kinds of mixes.

Where to Find a Bagel

You'll find Bagels in shelters, and some breeders do indeed breed them. Ask your veterinarian or other dog professionals if they know of a Bagel breeder near you. An Internet search will likely return restaurants, not dogs.

Chihchons (Chihuahuas + Bichons Frises)

A result of an effort to produce a small dog without an undercoat, the Chihchon is a dog that combines the compactness of the Chihuahua and the friendliness and coat characteristics of the Bichon Frise.

Breed Characteristics

Origin: United States

Coat: Preferably a single coat; wavy

Low allergy: Yes

Colors: Any color

Grooming needed: High; needs minimum weekly brushing and combing; regular trimming required

Trainability: Medium

Size: 6 to 12 inches, 4 to 15 pounds

Activity level: Low to medium

Good with other pets: Usually

Good with children: Good with older children

Health problems: Eye problems, patella luxation, Legg-Calve-Perthes disease, and hip dysplasia

Life span: 10 to 17 years

Registry: None

First generation or generational: First

Breed History

These dogs were no doubt a cross developed by breeders looking to create a small crossbreed with a single coat.

Meet the Chihchon

Bred to create a cute dog with a single coat, Chihchons might or might not be "allergy friendly," depending on whether the dog has a single or double coat.

Chihchons can be any color, but they often favor the lighter colors because Bichons are white.

Their temperament could be like both or either parent, Chihuahua or a Bichon.

Should you decide that the Chihchon is right for you, look for a breeder who breeds for temperament; screens for patella luxation, hip dysplasia, and Legg-Calve-Perthes disease; and screens for eye problems.

Where to Find a Chihchon

Ask your vet or other dog professionals who might be breeding Chihchons. You might be able to find some on the Internet, but like many of these breeds, they may be difficult to find.

> **Tip**
> Many crossbreed names aren't standardized, so you might see them written or spelled several ways. Asking for the mix (Chihuahua and Bichon Frise, for example) might make your search a little less frustrating.

Shihchons (or Bi-Tzus) (Shih Tzus + Bichons Frises)

The Shihchon is another crossbreed bred to create a toy dog with a single coat. These dogs have advantages over their Shih Tzu parents, as they might not have the health problems associated with a brachycephalic head.

Breed Characteristics

Origin: United States

Coat: Preferably a single coat; wavy

Low allergy: Yes

Colors: Any color

Grooming needed: High; needs minimum weekly brushing and combing; regular trimming required

Trainability: Medium

Size: 8 to 12 inches, 8 to 16 pounds

Activity level: Low to medium

Good with other pets: Usually

Good with children: Good with older children

Health problems: Eye problems, patella luxation, Legg-Calve-Perthes disease, and hip dysplasia

Life span: 10 to 15 years

Registry: None

First generation or generational: First

Breed History

These dogs were no doubt a cross developed by breeders looking to create a small crossbreed with a single coat.

Meet the Shihchon

Like the Chihchon, the Shihchon is one of many small or toy cross-breeds that appear from time to time. These dogs have single coats and, thus, are more likely to be appealing to allergy sufferers.

Shihchons can be any color, but they often favor the lighter colors because Bichons are white.

Should you decide that the Shihchon is right for you, look for a breeder who breeds for temperament; screens for patella luxation, hip dysplasia, and Legg-Calve-Perthes disease; and who screens for eye problems.

Where to Find a Shihchon

Ask your vet or other dog professionals who might be breeding Shihchons. You might be able to find some on the Internet, but like many of these breeds, they may be difficult to find.

Warning
Don't be taken in by a cute name. Be sure the dog you're getting is really something you want.

Pugles (Pugs + Beagles)

The Pugle is an adorable cross between a Pug and a Beagle. Part of the reason for crossing these two dogs is to avoid problems that the Pug has with his brachycephalic head, while still producing a cute dog.

Breed Characteristics

Origin: United States

Coat: Double coat; sheds

Low allergy: No

Colors: Black, fawn, tricolor, lemon and white, black and white, and red and white

Grooming needed: Medium; needs weekly brushing and combing

Trainability: Medium

Size: 10 to 16 inches, 14 to 30 pounds

Activity level: Low to medium

Good with other pets: Usually

Good with children: Good with older children

Health problems: Eye problems, patella luxation, Legg-Calve-Perthes disease, hip dysplasia, hypothyroidism, and epilepsy

Life span: 10 to 15 years

Registry: None

First generation or generational: First

Breed History

Pugles are a fairly new cross, probably intended to correct problems within the Pug breed.

Meet the Pugle

The Pugle is one of those whimsical crosses that creates an amusing dog. Don't look for a single coat with this crossbreed, because both the Beagle and the Pug are notorious shedders.

The Pugle can be any color of either breed.

Should you decide that the Pugle is right for you, look for a breeder who breeds for temperament; screens for patella luxation, hip dysplasia, Legg-Calve-Perthes disease, and hypothyroidism through OFA; and screens for eye problems through CERF. Pugs have notoriously bad hips, so this is very important. Ask if the Beagle lines have any sign of epilepsy.

Where to Find a Pugle

Ask your vet or other dog professionals who might be breeding Pugles. You might be able to find some on the Internet, but, like many of these breeds, they may be difficult to find.

> **Tip**
> Crossbreeds come and go depending on what people want. Most of the crossbreeds in this chapter are relatively new.

Bull Boxers (Boxers + Pit Bulls or Staffordshire Bull Terriers or Bull Dogs)

The Bull Boxer is a designer dog that originated in Great Britain in the 1990s. Originally a cross between a Boxer and a Staffordshire Bull Terrier, the idea was to create a sturdy dog who was both intelligent and social without the health or temperament problems sometimes associated with those breeds.

Breed Characteristics

Origin: Great Britain, 1990s

Coat: Short, smooth coat; average shedding

Low allergy: No

Colors: Fawn, bridle, white, red, and brown

Grooming needed: Low; bath and grooming when needed

Trainability: Moderate to high

Size: 16 to 23 inches, 35 to 60 pounds

Activity level: Medium

Good with other pets: Usually, requires socialization

Good with children: Usually, but needs supervision

Health problems: Patella luxation, hip dysplasia, cancers, skin problems, and heart problems

Life span: 10 to 15 years

Registry: None

First generation or generational: First

Breed History

The Bull Boxer was the result of an unplanned mating between a Staffordshire Bull Terrier and a Boxer in Great Britain sometime in the 1990s. Because the unplanned breeding produced such nice pups, the breeder decided to attempt the breeding again, and others followed suit. As the popularity increased, breeders tried other breedings such as Pit Bull and Boxer and Bull Dog and Boxer.

Meet the Bull Boxer

The Bull Boxer was bred to eliminate a number of problems associated with both parent breeds. They've inherited the friendliness of the Staffordshire but have less of a tendency to chase small animals. Some Bull Boxers can be aggressive if bred from poor lines or if poorly socialized.

Bull Boxers are touted as having great temperaments and are good with children, but be aware that discrepancies do exist, especially in dogs of mixed breeding, and any dog may bite if provoked. Therefore, it's very important that you screen for a dog or puppy with a good temperament and never leave small children alone with any dog.

Bull Boxers can be any color that comes from the Boxer or the Bull breed. Because they are almost exclusively bred first generation, they can look more like one or the other breed, depending on the genes.

Should you decide that the Bull Boxer is right for you, look for a breeder who breeds for temperament; screens for patella luxation and hip dysplasia; and screens for eye problems through.

Where to Find a Bull Boxer

No club is currently associated with Bull Boxers, so you're going to have to ask veterinarians, trainers, or groomers, or search on the Internet for possible Bull Boxer breeders.

The Least You Need to Know

- Most new crossbreeds provide variations and are good dogs for people looking for a companion.

- These crossbreeds are often "one-offs," which means you often have to do some searching either on the Internet or by asking around to find a breeder.

- Many of the smaller crossbreeds aren't suitable for very young children, who can easily hurt them by accident.

Chapter 10

Wolf Hybrids

In This Chapter

- 🏠 Learning what a wolf hybrid really is
- 🏠 Understanding why wolf (and wild canine) hybrids don't make the best pets
- 🏠 Realizing what life with a wolf hybrid is really like
- 🏠 Discovering what wolf hybrids are available

Wolf hybrids have been around for a long time, and despite frequent news reports about hybrid wolf attacks, many people think these crossbreeds make good pets.

In this chapter, you'll read about the wolf and other wild dog hybrids, and you'll learn whether or not this is really the kind of pet you want.

(Photo by Margaret H. Bonham)

Breed Characteristics

Origin: Varies

Crossbreed: Wolf and Alaskan Malamute, Siberian Husky, German Shepherd Dog, or any other domesticated breed

Coat: Double coat; shedding twice yearly

Low allergy: No

Colors: Gray, white, black, brown, or combination

Grooming needed: Medium; needs weekly brushing and combing, especially during twice-yearly seasonal shedding

Trainability: Low

Size: Varies: 22 to 30 inches at the shoulder, 60 to 100+ pounds

Activity level: High

Good with other pets: No

Good with children: No

Health problems: Hip dysplasia, elbow dysplasia, hypothyroidism, and eye problems

Life span: 8 to 13 years

Registry: None

First generation or generational: First; some generational

Breed History

The wolf hybrid is probably as old as the dog's history; however, some dog breeds have been bred from wolves in recent times, including Czech Wolfdogs, Saarloos Wolfhounds, and "Indian Dogs," which were bred from coyote-dog and wolf-dog crosses.

Meet the Wolf Hybrid

Do you really want a wolf hybrid? The concept of owning a wolf or wolf hybrid is a romantic notion, stirring up visions of the Wild West or the Klondike. Perhaps you've read Jack London's *White Fang* or one of his other stories. Perhaps you've talked with some breeders about wolves and wolf hybrids, and perhaps they've told you wolf hybrids are just dogs in wolf clothing. Is this true?

Not exactly. Wolf hybrids are hybrids in the true sense of the word, not just crossbreeds. Dogs are a subspecies of the wolf (hence dogs and wolves can breed and produce viable offspring who can reproduce), but a wolf isn't a dog, and a dog is not a wolf.

What separates the dog from the wolf is somewhere between 20,000 to 120,000 years of domestication and selective breeding. The genetics of the dog are different from those of the wolf; there's proof in the genes themselves.

One of the main differences between a dog and a wolf is that domestication has locked into the dog some traits you would see in an adolescent wolf. The dog is, in essence, the Peter Pan of wolves: the wolf who never grew up. This is known as *neoteny* (see Chapter 2), which enables the dog to bond with humans and to think of them as part of his pack.

Not Just a Wolfy-Looking Dog

What most people want when they get a wolf hybrid is Lassie in a wolf skin. The reality isn't so simple. If you've been reading about the complexity of dog genetics, you know you can't always predict complex traits. One complex trait is domestication.

Although there's no hard proof, it appears that "tameness" is associated with other traits such as floppy ears, different colors, and rounder heads, and experiments with breeding tameness in foxes seem to confirm this. Breeding a domesticated animal with a wild animal starts throwing a bunch of genes together—with unusual results!

Wolves are naturally wild and have certain natural instincts. Although wolves brought up from puppies can bond to humans, the bonding is a totally different type of bonding—not as a dog might bond to a human, but rather like a friend. A wolf does what a wolf does because he wants to—not because you tell him to. Training an independent spirit is precarious at best. You won't necessarily get the results you want.

For example, if a wolf wants to tear apart something—a bone, a stuffed animal, your shoes, or even your couch—he might simply go and do it. Correcting the wolf might be meaningless or might result in an angry wolf, or a wolf who holds a grudge. It won't change the outcome the next time, except maybe his reaction to you.

A wolf is a wild animal. A wolf hybrid is a wild animal who isn't afraid of people.

Temperament Problems

With a wolf hybrid, you get an unpredictable combination. Some wolf hybrids (usually those with less wolf heritage) can be very nice. Some with a high percentage of wolf heritage can be nice, too, but for the most part, they are completely unpredictable in temperament. All might be well for a while and then they might attack something or someone because of a particular trigger.

Wolf hybrids have very high prey drives. They will chase and possibly kill things that run from them, be it small animals like rabbits and mice or small pets like cats and small dogs. They could even prey on larger animals.

Did You Know?

Most hybrid breeders talk about percentages of wolf in their dogs. They get these percentages by breeding wolf to hybrids and hybrids to hybrids. A high-percentage hybrid is usually an animal with more than 70 percent wolf.

Does this mean you'll get a big bad wolf if you get a hybrid? Not necessarily, but most people are prepared for dealing with *dogs*, not with wolves. A dog's behavior isn't necessarily the same as a wolf's behavior, and without the proper socialization and training, the wolf hybrid could become difficult or even impossible to handle.

Experts often warn new pet owners to stay away from breeds such as Alaskan Malamutes and Siberian Huskies, among others, because of their independent qualities. Imagine a dog who is more difficult to deal with than those breeds. That's what you'd get with a wolf hybrid.

Warning

Like the wolf hybrids, coyote-dog crosses and dingo-dog crosses are difficult to handle and are not recommended as pets.

Don't get a wolf hybrid unless you're a very experienced canine handler—and even then, I don't recommend them. They need a lot of socialization and require a lot of attention, and you still have to treat them like the wild animal they are.

Unscrupulous Breeders

Unfortunately, plenty of unscrupulous breeders deal with wolf hybrids and wolf-hybrid look-alikes. Some breeders will call certain mixes wolf hybrids, even if the mixes don't have an ounce of wolf in them (not for the past 5,000 years, anyway!).

Other unscrupulous wolf hybrid breeders try to sell their hybrids as wolfy-looking dogs. Then, when the wolf hybrid puppy grows up and owners realize what they have, it becomes apparent that what they have isn't a dog, and the animal goes to the pound—or worse, is dumped out in the wild to fend for himself.

> **Warning**
> You might hear from someone how wonderful it is to own a wolf hybrid. The truth is that some unscrupulous breeders offer Husky-Malamute crosses, Malamute–German Shepherd crosses, or even purebred Alaskan Malamutes to buyers and claim that these dogs are wolf crosses. Although these dogs are infinitely easier to train, they are not wolf hybrids, despite the price.

Breed Bans and Insurance Problems

One huge problem with owning a wolf hybrid is liability. Several cities now have wolves and wolf hybrids on their list of banned animals, which makes it illegal for you to own them. Anyone who does faces a fine and could have their wolf hybrid taken away and presumably euthanized.

Many insurances won't cover households with wolves and wolf hybrids. For this reason, if your insurance carrier ever finds out you own such an animal, you could lose your homeowner's insurance.

If you're thinking of getting a wolf hybrid, you should probably contact your insurance carrier and check if they have any problems with that.

Where to Find a Wolf Hybrid

Finding a wolf hybrid breeder might be difficult, especially if your city bans them. Your best bet might be to ask veterinarians and trainers or look on the Internet.

The Least You Need to Know

- Wolves and wolf hybrids are not dogs because they lack the genetic domestication.

- Wolf hybrids should only be owned by the most experienced dog owners and trainers who are prepared for how difficult they can be.

- Often dogs sold as "wolf hybrids" are really dogs with little or no wolf in them.

- Many cities have outlawed wolf hybrids, and many insurance companies will not cover owners of wolf hybrids.

Part  3
Living With Your Designer Dog

You might be wondering how caring for a designer dog is different from caring for any other dog. Like other dogs, designer dogs do have health problems, need good nutrition, and require good training.

In Part 3, I cover some of the basics of designer dog ownership, from what to feed to how to train to whether you should breed your designer dog.

(Photo courtesy of Diana Peters Mayer)

11

Food for Thought: Nutrition

In This Chapter

- 🏠 Learning about good nutrition for your designer dog
- 🏠 Discovering types of dog foods—they're not all the same
- 🏠 Cooking for your designer dog
- 🏠 Understanding fad diets: healthy or hazardous?
- 🏠 Feeding the overweight designer dog

Nutrition is a hot topic among pet owners. Recently we've been bombarded with fad diets, raw diets, cooked diets, bone diets, and natural diets. Should you feed your designer dog a commercial dog food, or is that tantamount to abuse?

In this chapter, you'll learn about dog foods, how to spot a good premium brand of dog food, and what will work best for your designer dog, depending on his age and activity level. We'll look at pudgy pooches, too, and learn why you need to keep your dog trim.

Nutrition 101

You want the very best for your dog, but what should you feed him? Your dog gets his energy from the protein, fat, and carbohydrates in his food. Each of these nutrients is important for a healthy dog.

Protein

Protein is an essential nutrient. It provides 4 calories per gram and provides the building blocks for muscles, bone, organs, and connective tissue. It is the main component of enzymes, hormones, and antibodies. It helps with muscle repair, building and maintaining plasma volume and red blood cells, and building mitochondrial volume (energy burners) in working dogs.

The type of protein you feed your dog is very important. Dogs are carnivores and require complete proteins that are difficult to get from vegetable sources. Good sources of protein include meat (including chicken and poultry, meat meal, meat by-products, and meat by-product meals. Although we humans think that chowing down on lungs, hearts, and intestines is gross, our dogs love them, and they're actually good sources of protein.

Check the dog food label. The first ingredient should be the protein source, whether it's chicken, meat or chicken by-products, or another meat. Avoid dog foods with soy or meat meal and bone meal as the first protein source; both soy and bone meal are not as high quality and generally not as digestible as meat or meat by-products.

Warning _____

Should your dog be a vegetarian? No. Although dogs can and do subsist on vegetarian diets, dogs are designed to eat meat, not grains. Most vegetarian diets are based on soy protein, and soy can cause gas and bloating in dogs who are allergic to it. Your dog will do best on a meat-based dog food.

Fat

Fat is an energy-dense nutrient at 9 calories per gram. Good, high-quality fat sources include beef, poultry, and "animal fat," which may be a mixture of pork, beef, lamb, and horse fat. Animal fats tend to be better than vegetable fats in providing energy. Dogs and cats use fats that are commonly referred to as omega-6 long-chained fatty acids, which are usually a mixture of saturated (solid) and unsaturated (liquid) fats. Unsaturated fat tends to turn rancid more quickly than saturated fat.

Carbohydrates

Carbohydrates provide 4 calories per gram of energy and are useful for fiber and extra energy in your dog's diet. In working dogs, a carbohydrate snack can help refuel his cells after sustained exercise.

Most dogs benefit from cooked grains, which are easier to digest. Carbohydrates in the form of fiber help keep your dog's colon healthy, and it helps in water absorption.

Feeding Your Designer Dog

Feeding a dog, designer or otherwise, used to be no big deal. You went to the store, picked up a bag of Canine Crunchies, and poured it into a bowl. What could be simpler? Nowadays, you've probably heard from someone, somewhere (probably the Internet) that you could cause your dog to develop cancer, allergies, autoimmune diseases, and who knows what else, if you feed him anything that comes out of a bag.

But is this right? Will you really kill your dog if you feed him commercial food? Is the food at the grocery store okay for him? And what about bones?

First, you need to understand that good nutrition for dogs isn't as easy as tossing him a meaty bone. Nor is it just giving him a bit of hamburger, cooked rice, and raw veggies. Dogs need a specific amount of protein and fat and a special balance of nutrients to live. You can cause a serious imbalance simply by feeding your dog the wrong things.

The American Association of Feed Control Officials (AAFCO) has determined the minimum nutrition a dog needs to be healthy. To have a complete and balanced diet, dog food with an AAFCO statement must meet or exceed the standards set forth by AAFCO. Otherwise, the diet can't be labeled as complete and balanced.

Plenty of dog foods and treats aren't complete and balanced, so you must always look for the AAFCO statement on the label. Even then, be aware that this is only a guarantee that the food meets the minimums so your dog won't have a serious health problem associated with the food's nutrition. An AAFCO statement doesn't guarantee the quality of the ingredients.

The good news is that some commercial foods are really good for your dog. Dog food manufacturers have spent millions of dollars on research to determine the optimum nutrition for your dog. The dog foods available today are better than dog foods 20, 10, or even 5 years ago.

Did You Know?

The words *premium* and *super premium* are tough to define when it comes to dog food—mostly because the Food and Drug Administration (FDA) and AAFCO have no definition of premium food. In fact, *premium* and *super premium* are marketing words and might not fit the actual dog food.

The bad news is that there's still a lot of "junk" dog food. This food tends to be cheap and has fillers, sugar, and artificial colors. It's the food you'd normally see priced at a deep discount when compared to other dog food. This dog food may have an attractive price, but the digestibility of the nutrients is lower than that of premium food, so you must feed more of a cheaper food to obtain the same amount of nutrition a premium food contains.

Your dog might have to eat twice or more of a cheaper brand dog food as he would a premium brand dog food. (And the cheaper brand dog food ends up as more poop in your yard instead of good nutrition for your dog.)

So bargain brands aren't much of a bargain. Sure, you save $10 to $20 on a bag of food, but instead of feeding 2 or 3 cups, you have to feed 5 to 7. That's quite a difference!

The bargain brands used to be anything you can buy at a grocery store, but that's really not true anymore. Some grocery store chains actually carry some decent food. So how do you know a premium dog food when you see it?

Finding a Premium Dog Food

When searching for a premium dog food, look at the label. The ingredients are listed in descending order of total weight, with the most abundant ingredient listed first. The first ingredient should be an animal protein (meat, poultry, fish, eggs, or dairy). The next ingredient may be a carbohydrate source such as corn, rice, or wheat, but be careful! If the label lists several carbohydrate sources in a row, those can actually outweigh the protein source and the food may be more grain than meat.

You can also contact the manufacturer directly. Most manufacturers have toll-free numbers on their packaging for questions, and many have Internet sites as well. You can find out through the manufacturer what the *digestibility* of the dog food is. If it's more than 80 percent, you can assume it's a premium dog food.

Purchase a recognizable brand or one you can get readily. If the local pet boutique where you usually buy your dog's food is closed, you need to be able to get the food somewhere else if you run out.

Definition

Digestibility refers to the percentage of nutrients in a dog food that the dog can use after it is digested.

Palatability is also very important. All that good nutrition is worthless if your dog doesn't eat it. So find something he likes to eat, and stick with it.

Mixing Foods

Should you feed your dog just one brand of food, or should you mix two or more foods? Experts often recommend feeding only one brand of dog food and continuing with it. However, some vets and nutritionists dispute this and recommend that you choose a few pet foods and rotate them, the thought being that if one food lacks something, it will be balanced by the other food(s).

But there are some fallacies to this line of thought:

- The dog food is either complete and balanced or it isn't. If you believe the feeding trials, research, and analysis that show the food to be complete, then your dog doesn't need anything else. Is it optimum? There's room for debate there.

- Research has shown that dogs need a minimum of six weeks or more on the same dog food before you can see any benefit from the food. Constantly rotating pet foods will provide nutrition, but there's really no way to tell what is helping and what isn't.

- Changing foods frequently can cause gastric upsets, including diarrhea. In some cases, it can cause bloat, a life-threatening disease.

> **Tip**
>
> If you switch or rotate your dog's food, do it gradually to prevent diarrhea, stomach upsets, and bloat. Start with 10 percent of the new food and 90 percent of the old food the first day. Then, each day, increase the new food and decrease the old food, each by 10 percent, until you're feeding 100 percent of the new food.

If you do decide to rotate foods, be sure to mix the food or change one food over to another gradually.

Canned, Dry, Frozen, or Semi-Moist?

Dog food comes in a variety of forms, the most common being dry and canned. Most owners like to use dry dog food and mix in one of the other foods to make the dry food more palatable. What's right for your dog? Here's how the foods stack up:

- **Dry dog food.** Pound for pound, dry dog food or kibble is the most cost-effective dog food. You have more choices in dry dog food than in any other food.

- **Canned dog food.** Canned dog food is very palatable, but it can be expensive. As a treat for their dog, many owners like to add a can to their dog's dry food.

- **Semi-moist food.** Semi-moist food is chock full of colors, preservatives, and sugar—and it's expensive. Use semi-moist food sparingly or as treats, if at all.

- **Frozen food.** Frozen food usually contains no preservatives, but it must be kept frozen to avoid bacterial growth or spoilage. It's expensive, too—you're paying for both water weight and freezer storage.

- **Compressed meat rolls.** These are highly palatable, expensive, and need to be refrigerated once open.

Tip

Feed your dog regular, measured meals instead of free feeding him. One benefit of feeding meals is that you can see right away if he's sick. If your dog is normally a good eater and suddenly skips a meal, it might be a sign of illness.

Designer Dog Foods?

The latest in dog food nutrition is customized food for your particular breed or size of dog. Some dog food manufacturers have realized that not all dogs are the same and have different nutritional requirements depending on age, activity level, and breed.

Some dog food manufacturers have actually created dog food for specific breeds, such as German Shepherd Dogs or Labrador Retrievers. While this doesn't necessarily help the crossbreed owner, you might consider one of these foods if your dog is more like one of the breeds than the other. For example, if you have a Poo dog, you might want to consider a Poodle formula for your dog.

What Food to Feed *Your* Dog

Use these guidelines when selecting a dry dog food for your designer dog:

- 🏠 If your designer dog is under 12 months of age, he needs a premium puppy food. Most puppy foods have at least 28 percent protein/17 percent fat by weight content.

- 🏠 If your designer dog is an active adult, he needs a premium active adult food that has approximately 25 percent protein/ 15 percent fat by weight content.

- 🏠 If your designer dog is overweight or inactive, he needs a maintenance or "light" version of a premium adult food.

- 🏠 If your designer dog works (agility, flyball, sledding), he needs a premium performance dog food that's approximately 30 percent protein/20 percent fat by weight content.

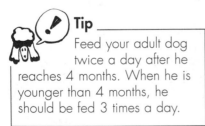

Tip

Feed your adult dog twice a day after he reaches 4 months. When he is younger than 4 months, he should be fed 3 times a day.

🏠 If your designer dog is a senior (over 8 years), he needs a dog food that maintains his weight and energy level. Don't switch him to a senior-type dog food unless he's gaining weight or has some under-lying health problem.

🏠 You can use the appropriate breed formula, provided it maintains a healthy weight on your designer dog.

Did You Know?

If you like gadgets, you'll like the automatic pet feeder. Battery operated, the pet feeder can feed your dog on schedule when you're not home. An ice pack and two compartments keep food fresh.

Home Cooking for Your Dog

Raw foods seem to be all the rage, and it's trendy to feed them to your dog, but are they really a good idea?

Yes and no. A homemade diet has several benefits, but there are plenty of reasons not to feed your dog this diet as well. Let's look at both.

First, understand that I am lumping homemade and raw diets together because most raw diets are homemade except for those that are AAFCO approved and sold commercially as frozen dog food (above). There are differences where some homemade diets are actually cooked, so some of the statements may not quite fit.

What the Doggie Chefs Say

Most people who feed raw diets cite a number of reasons why you shouldn't feed a commercial diet. Most of the reasons sound good, but a number of fallacies associated with their statements do exist:

🏠 **I prefer to feed an all-natural diet free of preservatives and chemicals.** This is a very tough thing to do. The main preser-vative culprit is fat—which turns rancid very quickly when exposed to air. Animal fats—a preferred source of energy—are almost always preserved with BHT, BHA, or some other preservative. Even if you manage to eliminate the preservatives, your pet is still exposed to chemicals due to antibiotics and other medications in the food animals, unless you choose completely organic meats, and even then, there are chemicals in the environment.

I know what ingredients I'm giving my dog. Yes, that's true, but do you know the amounts of protein, fats, vitamins, and minerals you're feeding him?

Raw bones are safe for dogs to eat. Actually, they're not. Veterinarians have operated on dogs who have eaten raw bones, to remove blockages and fix perforated intestines. Any bone that your dog can swallow whole can cause a problem.

Raw food diets mimic what dogs eat in the wild. Again, no, they don't. When wolves kill their prey, they eat the stomach contents of a ruminant (partially digested plants); the skin and hair; the organ meats, including the liver, lungs, stomach, intestines, spleen, heart, and connecting tissue; and the muscle meat and bones. This doesn't equal green beans, lettuce, and a chicken wing! Wolves also don't live long in the wild—most barely make it past 8 years.

Dogs' intestines can handle bacteria in raw diets. Dogs seem to be more resistant to nasty bacteria than humans, but that means they're carrying around that bacteria and can give it to you. Younger and older dogs tend to be more susceptible to these bacteria and can die from infections.

I know how to feed my kids—so why can't I formulate a dog food? Feeding kids and feeding dogs are two different things. When you feed your kids, do you let them eat vitamin-fortified cereal? Do they drink milk (enriched with vitamin D)? Do you use iodized salt? Do you give your kids vitamins? A lot of the work has been done for you already when it comes to proper nutrition for your family. Dogs require special nutrition, too, and not something you give your kids. Dogs need nutrition formulated for their bodies just as your kids need nutrition formulated for theirs.

🏠 **The ingredients I use are better and fresher than what's in dog food.** Maybe, but fresh food without preservatives tends to spoil faster.

You must be careful about E. coli, campylobacter, and salmonella poisoning. If you cook the food, cooking can destroy vital nutrients you might be depending on for adequate nutrition.

🏠 **My dog can't get the nutrition he needs from commercial dog food.** Unless your dog is sick and needs a special diet (and there are many veterinary diets available), or if he is an endurance working dog (such as a sled dog), your dog will get all the nutrition he needs from a premium or super-premium dog food.

🏠 **Feeding raw foods will make my dog healthier.** Maybe— or it could make him sick. You should never, under any circumstance, feed your dog certain foods, such as onions, grapes, and raw salmon. Raw salmon from the Northwest may contain a fluke that can be poisonous to your dog, onions can cause anemia, and grapes and raisins can cause renal failure. Raw game meat can contain tularemia, trichinosis, and tapeworms. There's also the potential for food poisoning due to campylobacter, salmonella, and E. coli.

Difficulties Balancing Nutrients

AAFCO has set forth the minimum guidelines for dog foods. Unless you are a veterinary nutritionist, how close do you think you can come to balancing nutrients in your kitchen? For example, calcium and phosphorus require a special ratio of about 1.5:1. If phosphorus exceeds that ratio (as in a diet with too much meat), your dog's body will pull calcium from his bones, making them brittle.

The truth is most raw diets and home-cooked diets are deficient in some vitamins, are improperly balanced in certain nutrients, or have dangerous levels of bacteria that may or may not hurt your dog, but may hurt *you*. Dogs who look good on these diets now might have long-lasting deficiencies that might affect their long-term health. Most people who concoct these diets don't have the knowledge or expertise needed to do it properly.

If you want to feed your designer dog a raw food diet or a home-cooked diet, contact a veterinary college and speak with a nutritionist there. Most will be able to recommend and analyze diets for deficiencies and help you formulate a correct diet for your pet.

Performance Diets: Feeding the Canine Athlete

If your designer dog works hard, such as in sledding, agility, flyball, or other work, he should be on a super-premium performance blend of dog food because more protein and fat are necessary for hard-working dogs to maintain muscle mass and keep their weight.

Warning

Stress diarrhea and bloody diarrhea can be signs of more serious problems such as parvovirus, distemper, coronavirus, cancer, bowel irritation, or bacterial infections. Have your veterinarian rule these out in your dog.

When you choose a high-performance dog food, find one that is highly digestible. Otherwise, you may see stress diarrhea or even bloody diarrhea. Some cheaper brands of dog food have rough-cut grains that can irritate your dog's bowels and cause bleeding. If you see blood in your dog's stool, have your vet check out your dog to rule out other causes. If your dog is in good shape, try mixing water with his food, changing dog foods, or adding canned dog food to his diet to help cushion the food as it passes through his intestines.

You must be careful when feeding performance foods, though, because the tendency is to feed too much and your dog will become fat.

Fad Diets

The term *fad diets* tends to conjure up magazine ads that promise you 50 pounds of weight loss in 3 days—and they're just about as unhealthy! Avoid feeding your dog diets that have strange or unusual ingredients or that aren't formulated to AAFCO guidelines. These diets aren't complete and balanced, and may cause severe nutritional deficiencies.

Junk Food: Between-Meal Snacks

How can anyone resist those eyes? In-between meal snacks will happen no matter how careful you are, so choose judiciously. Lean pieces of meat, raw vegetables, and crunchy biscuits are all good snacks.

Even so, you should keep all snacks to 10 percent of all your dog's calories (including the occasional piece of pizza, table scraps, or potato chips you "accidentally" slipped to him). Plus, table scraps can turn your dog into a picky eater. Most are high in calories, salt, carbohydrates, and fats and have little nutritional value beyond calories.

> **Tip**
> To teach good eating habits, put down your dog's bowl with his food and set a timer for 10 minutes. At the end of 10 minutes, pick up his food bowl if he hasn't touched it, and don't give him his food until his next scheduled meal. After a few rounds of this, your dog will learn that feeding time means it's time to eat.

Poisonous Temptations: Chocolate and Other Unsafe Foods

Not everything is safe for your dog to eat. Some foods are poisonous to your dog. These include the following:

- **Alcohol.** Even a small amount can cause alcohol poisoning. *A drunk dog is not funny,* and a small amount can be extremely toxic.

- **Chocolate.** Contains theobromine, a substance that's poisonous to dogs. Dark or bittersweet chocolate is more poisonous than milk chocolate.

- **Grapes and raisins.** These can cause renal failure in dogs.

- **Onions.** Might cause anemia.

- **Raw salmon from the Northwest.** Contains a parasite that can kill your dog.

- **Coffee.** Can be poisonous to dogs.

Obesity

As it is in humans, obesity is a common problem in dogs. Some owners are heavy-handed with the treats and the dog food measuring cup, and others don't exercise their dogs regularly.

Obesity can lead to health problems in your dog, just as it can in humans. You can help extend your dog's life by keeping him trim and fit.

Is Your Dog Svelte or Swelled?

Weight isn't a good indicator of fitness, as different dogs have different builds. Instead, you should examine your dog to determine his fitness. You should be able to put your thumbs on your dog's spine and feel his ribs. If you can't feel his ribs, or if you can barely feel them under a thick layer of padding, your dog is too fat. If you can see your dog's ribs and pelvic bones, he's too thin.

Diet Isn't a Four-Letter Word

If your dog needs to shed a few pounds, talk with your vet about putting your dog on a diet and exercise program. Most vets are able to prescribe a diet food that will help shed the pounds. You can also try the maintenance or light version of your dog's food.

If your dog is the quintessential couch potato, getting him off the couch and into an exercise regimen will help shave off unwanted pounds. If you and your dog are exercising to shed weight, remember the following rules:

- **Start slow.** Your dog is probably out of shape and needs to build up to rigorous exercise.

- **Choose a fun activity you both can do.** Playing fetch, jogging, and dog sports are possible activities.

- **Be careful when exercising when it's hot.** Overweight dogs tend to overheat faster.

> **Tip**
> Use the feeding guidelines on the dog food label as a guideline and adjust accordingly. Most dog food manufacturers recommend larger portions than your dog actually needs.

The Least You Need to Know

- Feed your dog a premium dog food that meets or exceeds AAFCO standards in accordance with your dog's age and activity level.

- Not all dog foods are the same. Bargain brands tend to be no bargain because they have more fillers and are less digestible than premium brands.

🏠 Homemade diets can be tricky to balance and may cause malnutrition. Some raw diets may contain salmonella and E. coli. A veterinary nutritionist at a veterinary college can help you develop a complete and balanced diet.

🏠 Limit snacks and treats to no more than 10 percent of your dog's total diet.

🏠 Your dog is obese if you can't feel his ribs or can barely feel them under a layer of fat. Contact your vet for recommendations regarding a weight loss and exercise program.

Chapter 12

Grooming Your Designer Dog

In This Chapter

- 🐾 Checking out the designer dog coat
- 🐾 Grooming your designer dog
- 🐾 Looking for a professional groomer

You want to keep your designer dog looking great, so in this chapter, I cover everything you need to know, from understanding your designer dog's coat, to grooming your dog, to finding the best groomer who will take care of your baby.

The Designer Dog's Coat

What often attracts people to designer dogs is their apparently no-shed coats, but let's bust that myth right now. There isn't a completely shed-free dog. Even the Chinese Crested, who is virtually hairless, sheds a bit of hair from the top of his head.

Many designer dogs have single coats or open coats—that is, a coat without an undercoat. That single coat grows like human hair, and these dogs still lose hair as new follicles grow. The difference is that they don't have a once- or twice-a-year seasonal shed like many double-coated breeds do, so you'll have less shedding to deal with.

Did You Know?

A warm (not hot!) bath will facilitate shedding and make it easier for you to get rid of the loose hair on your dog.

However, not all crossbreed dogs with a single coat will produce offspring with a single coat every time—especially if one of the parents has a double coat. Depending on the genetics and which genes went into the particular dog, a designer dog touted as no-shed could, indeed, shed.

Single Versus Double Coat

So if a single coat means less shedding, does that mean less maintenance? No, and in fact, most dogs with single coats require *more* grooming than double-coated dogs. Because the hair is continuously growing, it requires constant trimming and scissoring.

If your designer dog has a single coat, you'll have to learn how to maintain it properly, or it will tangle and mat. A mat is a clump of hair that tangles due to some dirt or loose hair. Think of how some children's hair can tangle, and multiply it by a hundred or more. As an adolescent, your single-coat designer dog may have to be brushed every day until he has his adult coat, then you'll need to properly maintain his coat. That means learning how to trim using an electric trimmer and scissors.

Dogs with double coats have a top coat and a downy undercoat. Depending on the breeds crossed and the climate, the double-coat dog may shed seasonally once or twice a year, or he may shed year-round. A double-coat dog may require a fair amount of brushing and combing, or may be "wash and wear," depending on the length of his coat.

No Guarantees

So what kind of coat does your designer dog have? If you have a dog who is a crossbreed with a single-coat breed, such as a Poodle, Bichon Frise, or Yorkshire Terrier, you might have a dog with a single coat, especially if the parent dogs had single coats. However, if your dog comes from crossbreeds with double coats—or one with a double coat—you might have a double-coat dog. The type of grooming depends a lot on the type of coat your puppy inherits.

No one can guarantee what kind of coat the crossbreeds will have when genetics often throw in interesting combinations. In fact, purebreds sometimes have incorrect coats even though they've been bred for many generations with correct coats. (The breed standards of all breeds specify what is a correct coat and what is not.)

Seasonal Shedding

Even with a designer dog, you might still have to deal with seasonal shedding (that is, shedding twice a year, usually during spring and fall). Brushing out the dead fur will actually make your dog more comfortable and less likely that his fur will mat.

Some people resort to shaving their dogs in the summertime, but this isn't necessarily a good idea. When you shave your dog, you re-move the protective top coat as well as the undercoat and expose your dog to the sun (and to sunburn!). A dog with a well-maintained coat is actually cooler than one who has been shaved.

Grooming Your Designer Dog

How often do you have to groom your designer dog? That depends on the coat type. For dogs with open, single, or Poodle-type coats, trimming to the proper cut and bathing and trimming monthly for maintenance, with frequent brushings in between, will probably do. Dogs with double coats require frequent brushing during their shedding periods.

Tools of the Trade

You'll need some standard supplies for grooming your dog. These include the basic brushes and combs, but also items that might seem extravagant, such as a dog blow dryer and grooming table. These items will make your job much easier, though.

Here's what to stock your dog grooming "salon" with:

- Blow dryer for dogs (not human blow dryers—they're too hot and could burn your dog's skin)

- Electric clipper (for single-coat dogs)

- Flea comb

- Grooming table with noose (this restraint will hold your dog in place and will save your back; *never* leave your dog unattended on it though!)

- Long-tooth comb

- Mat splitter or mat rake (for double-coat dogs)

- Nail clippers or nail grinder

- Shampoo and conditioner formulated for dogs

- Shears (for single-coat dogs)

- Slicker brush (a brush with soft wire bristles that traps loose hair and helps remove the dead hair)

- Styptic powder (to stop the bleeding if you cut into the nail quick)

- Thinning shears (for single-coat dogs)

- Toothpaste and toothbrush formulated for dogs

Tip

You can vacuum away hair from your dog with a specially designed vacuum attachment. It's made to brush and vacuum away loose dog hair.

🏠 Undercoat rake (for double-coat dogs)

🏠 Zoom Groom or Curry Brush (for short-coat dogs)

Brushing and Combing

Brushing a dog's coat will keep the dog's skin and hair healthy. How you brush your dog depends on the coat, but you should start by brushing the hair and untangling any mats. (Use a mat splitter or a detangler solution.) Never use scissors to cut out a mat! You can severely cut your dog's skin, even if you are careful. If your dog has too many mats, bring him to a groomer who might have to use clippers to cut away the matted fur.

Next, brush your dog's hair against the lay of the hair. This helps stimulate oils in the coat. Then, brush the dog's hair back the "right" way.

Bathing

Although it's tempting, you should never bathe a dog without first brushing him out. Some designer dogs are prone to tangles, and their hair will mat worse if you bathe them without brushing first.

You might want to put a small piece of cotton in your dog's ears so the water doesn't get in them. Be certain, too, the water is tepid to the touch.

Use a good pH-balanced shampoo especially made for dogs. Do not use products made for humans; they can dry out a dog's skin. Follow with a conditioner made for dogs, and rinse thoroughly—any remaining shampoo or conditioner will attract dirt.

Tip
Some dogs hate baths. If yours does, get a restraining noose that attaches via suction cup so you can keep him in the tub while you wash him. Never leave a dog unattended in a noose, or he might strangle.

After rinsing, pat down your dog with thick towels to get rid of the excess water, and keep him away from drafts. Use a dog blow dryer to dry your dog—don't use a human hair dryer, as these are too hot and will burn your dog's skin and scorch his fur.

Trimming

Unless you're a pro at clipping, you might want to leave the clipping to a professional who can shape your dog's coat into a nice style. The groomer can show you how to maintain the cut between grooming sessions.

If you plan to learn how to clip your dog's fur, ask an expert. Some trainers and groomers will be happy to help you. If you want your pet to look like a show dog, consider asking breeders and people who show their single-coat dogs what cut would work with your dog's coat.

Nail Clipping

Clip your dog's nails once a week, using one of two types of dog nail clippers: the guillotine variety and the one with a scissor handle. Both work well.

When trimming your dog's nails, only cut the nail portion, and be very careful about cutting the *quick* (the fleshy part that supplies blood to the nail). You can see the quick in white nails as a fleshy pink part. If you cut the quick, you'll cause your dog pain, and it will bleed profusely. To stop the bleeding, pack the nail with styptic powder.

If your dog has black nails, trim a little at the ends and leave it at that. You can't see the quick in black nails. If it feels spongy, stop. Otherwise, you'll have to have an expert cut them.

Getting Your Designer Dog a Designer 'Do

At this point, the thought of trimming and keeping his coat just right may be daunting to you. Or maybe you just don't have the time to mess with it. If the grooming thing isn't for you, there's no shame in having a professional handle it.

Taking your dog to a professional groomer at least once a month will help keep most adult coats under control. For adolescents and dogs with especially difficult coats, you may take your dog in for weekly or bi-monthly brushing and combing, or bathing and trimming once a month.

Finding a Professional Groomer

How do you find the best groomer around? The best thing to do is to ask your dog-owning friends where they take their dogs. A good referral is hard to beat, and if they're happy with the groomer they're using, the groomer is likely to do a good job on your designer dog as well.

If none of your friends use groomers or don't have any recommendations, try contacting your vet. Some veterinary clinics have groomers associated with their practice. You can also check the Yellow Pages and Internet for dog groomers in your area.

Here are some basic questions to ask a prospective groomer:

- What are your certifications? (Certifications aren't necessary, but they mean the groomer has met certain criteria.)
- What services do you perform? (Clean ears? Express anal sacs? Clip toenails?)
- How many clients do you have?
- Do you have references?

- Do you tranquilize? (This is not advisable, especially for dogs who have seizures.)

- Are you familiar with my kind of designer dog?

Once you've prescreened the groomer, it's time to visit his or her shop. If the groomer is busy on the day you visit, you're likely to see hair and water on the floor, but the shop should still be neat and orderly. Watch how the groomer and her staff (if any) handle the dogs. Is the groomer gentle or rough? If she uses cage dryers, does she check on the animals frequently? Does the groomer have enough cages to contain all the dogs comfortably?

If everything looks okay and the references check out, try the groomer. Don't just choose a groomer based on price alone without checking out the shop and his or her manner with the dogs—your dog will be in that person's care.

Do-It-Yourself Dog Washes

One popular alternative to taking your dog to a professional groomer is a do-it-yourself dog wash. These places (some of them in big-name pet supply stores) charge you $8 to $15 and provide water, towels, shampoo, grooming implements, a groomer-style tub to wash your dog, and doggie hair dryers to dry them.

The Least You Need to Know

- Designer dogs aren't necessarily shed free. Much depends on the combination of genetics.

- Always brush out mats before bathing a dog. Never clip them out with scissors.

- Ask your dog-owning friends or veterinarian whom they might recommend as a groomer.

- A groomer can bathe, brush, and clip your designer dog.

Exercise, Play, and Training

In This Chapter

- 🏠 Housetraining your dog

- 🏠 Teaching your dog clicker training

- 🏠 Learning how to teach your dog commands: "Sit," "Down," "Stay," "Heel," "Come," and "Walk on a Leash"

- 🏠 Getting the lowdown on the high-tech training

- 🏠 Picking the best toys for your dog

In this chapter, I cover housetraining and the basic obedience commands: "Sit," "Down," "Stay," "Heel," "Come," and "Walk on a Leash." We'll also look at some high-tech training aids and find out what toys and chews are good to give your designer dog.

Housetraining

Housetraining (or housebreaking) is the one training you must do right. Your dog might never learn to properly sit or lie down and will still remain a happy pet, but if your dog is constantly using your home as his toilet, you're not going to put up with that for long. Housetraining takes time. It's not something a puppy can learn in a week (despite the claims of some books), although an adult dog may be more reliable.

Did You Know?

A crates simulates the dog's den in the wild.
All dogs have a denning instinct. Your dog or puppy will be happier if he has a "den" all his own.

To aid in housetraining, one thing you'll need to purchase is a crate, if you don't already have one. (Some people call it a cage, but this is an erroneous connotation.) The crate will contain your puppy when you can't watch him. Dogs (and puppies) won't soil their den area, and you'll use this basic instinct to housetrain your puppy or dog.

There are basically two types of crates: wire crates and the molded type required for shipping by the airlines. Both are good for crate training. Be sure to get a crate that's just big enough for your dog to stand up, turn around, and lie down in comfortably. You might have to buy a bigger crate as she grows up, or you can buy a crate at his adult size and cordon off the excess space (otherwise he'll make a mess in the crate and stay in the clean part).

Get your puppy or dog used to his crate by tossing in treats. Give him his toys in his crate and feed him his meals in it, too. Slowly extend the time he spends in the crate so it becomes a place of good things and security—never a bad place to stay.

Warning _____

Puppies who come from pet stores and puppy mills are often forced to relieve themselves in their crate, thereby rendering the crate useless as a training method. If this is the case with your puppy, you'll have to work extra hard at teaching him to go outside or consult with an animal behaviorist.

You'll need to keep your puppy on a schedule when crating him. When you can't watch him, he should be in the crate with the door closed. The daily schedule for letting the puppy out to relieve himself should look something like this:

- First thing in the morning
- After breakfast
- Before you go to work or school
- Lunchtime
- Before you go back to work or school
- When you get home from work or school
- After playtime
- After dinner
- After playtime
- Before bedtime

Puppies cry at night and when they're left alone in the crate, but you can mitigate some of that:

- Place your puppy's crate in your bedroom so he can sleep in the same room as you.
- Try a SnugglePuppie, a cute stuffed dog with a heartbeat and warming pad to simulate your pup's mom. For more information, go to www.snugglepuppys.com.

Some babies fall asleep when you sing them lullabies, and your puppy likely will, too. Audio-Therapy Innovations offers *Canine Lullaby* CDs, which uses heartbeat and music therapy to calm human babies. Go to www.caninelullabies.com.

You should always let your puppy outside to relieve himself after he eats or drinks, after he plays, and after naps. When he goes outside, praise him.

What if he goes in the house? If you "catch him in the act," make a noise to startle him and whisk him outside to go. Be patient—you've startled him, after all! When he does finally finish his business outside, praise him. Then, go inside and clean up the mess with soap and water, and follow it up with a solution of white vinegar and water or an enzymatic cleaner specially formulated for cleaning up pet messes. Stay away from fancy household cleaners. Most use ammonia—the same chemical that's in urine.

> **Warning**
> Never leave a puppy younger than 6 months of age in a crate longer than 4 hours. Never leave an adult dog in a crate longer than 9 hours.

Clicker Training for Designer Dogs

Clicker training is a method of positive training that's taken the animal training world by storm. It's a form of *operant conditioning*, meaning that the dog learns behaviors by experiencing the consequences of certain actions. Operant conditioning is how most animals, and even people, learn. On the positive side of operant conditioning, the animal does something and receives a reward. On the negative side, the animal does something and receives a punishment.

> **Did You Know?**
> Clicker training has been promoted by notable trainers such as Karen Pryor and Gary Wilkes.

Clicker training uses primarily *positive reinforcement*—that is, the animal does something and receives a reward. With the clicker, you teach your dog to associate the sound of the click with a treat. When your dog does something right, you click and then give him a treat. When he performs a behavior you don't want, you ignore it, and he receives no reward.

Definition _____

Operant conditioning is a learning method by which the animal learns from the consequences of his actions, both good and bad. **Positive reinforcement** is a training method by which desirable behavior is rewarded. The opposite of positive reinforcement, *negative reinforcement* punishes for undesirable behavior.

Clicking works much the same as praise does, although instead of saying "Good dog!" you click. Click, treat. Click, treat. Your dog will associate the correct action (the one you clicked for) with the treat. Eventually, he'll learn that the click means "You did it right!" even when there's no treat forthcoming.

You might have so much fun with the clicker, you'll forget you're even training your dog. If this happens, don't worry! You're both enjoying yourselves.

Introducing the Clicker

Introduce the clicker while your dog isn't doing anything in particular, preferably before his feeding time when he's a bit hungry. Have plenty of treats on hand, then show him the clicker. Click and give him a treat. If your dog is startled by the noise, try muffling it a bit in your hand when you click.

Click and give him a treat. Click, treat. Click, treat. You might have to do this for a bit, but at some point your dog will start picking up that when he hears a click, he's going to get a treat. When you click, he should look expectantly at you for the treat.

Sometimes it takes a while for the dog to make the association. This is okay. If, after 5 minutes or so, you haven't made any progress, put away the clicker and play with your dog. Try again tomorrow.

> **Did You Know?** _____
>
> Why bother using the clicker at all? The clicker is a way to mark the desirable behavior. While yes, you can use your voice, quite often your timing isn't going to be as effective as a clicker. While you're still trying to say "Good," you could've clicked and treated. Because our dogs hear our voices so much, sometimes they tune us out. The clicker establishes a very definite means of communicating that the action you clicked for was the right action.

Once your dog has figured out that treats come right after clicks, the next step is to vary the time between the click and the treat and also where he receives the treat. This will teach your dog that he can expect a treat even if it's a little delayed or if it might not be in your hand, but tossed on the ground. (Remember, your dog must first associate the click with the treat before you proceed to this next step.)

Click and silently count to five. Your dog might look expectantly at you or even drool a bit before you give him the treat. When you get to five, give him the treat. Now click again, and silently count to three, then treat him. Now click and silently count to 10, then treat. If he gets insistent or pushy, don't do anything. Just wait until he stops before you give him the treat. His correct response is to wait patiently until he gets the treat.

Once he's used to varying times, click and toss the treat in front of him. If he has problems finding the treat, show it to him and tell him "Good dog!" when he picks it up. Once he figures out that the treat doesn't have to come from your hand, click and toss the treat somewhere else.

Introducing the Target Stick

Along with the clicker, you can use a target stick to get your dog's attention and lead him to further training. After he's mastered click and treat, hold the target stick out for your dog to sniff. If he touches the stick, click and treat. You might have to wiggle the stick a bit to get him interested in it. Even if he accidentally touches it, click and treat.

Suppose your dog doesn't touch the stick? Well, you can start by *shaping* the behavior. Shaping is a fancy term for teaching the behavior you want in small increments. For example, click and treat every time your dog looks at the stick. Then, after he looks at the stick and waits for you to click, wait and see what he does next. He might stare at it longer or perhaps nudge or paw the stick. If he needs encouragement, wave the stick close to him, but don't touch the stick to him—instead, let your dog touch the stick. Then click and treat.

Once your dog touches the stick, hears a click, and gets a treat, he might be puzzled. After all, he's been doing nothing to get a click and treat, but now he has to work for it. Offer the stick again and see if your dog will touch the stick (accidentally or on purpose). When he does, click and treat.

Definition

Shaping is a training method that starts with a basic behavior that's relatively easy to learn and slowly progressing in increments to the behavior you want. Teaching a dog to touch something with his paw can be shaped to waving good-bye, closing or opening a door, or other behaviors by clicking at incremental steps until the dog displays the final desired behavior. A **cue** is a word or signal a dog is supposed to associate with a particular behavior.

Some dogs quickly learn to touch the target stick. Others take time and you might have to have several sessions before your dog starts touching the target stick. Once he touches it consistently, start using a *cue* word such as "Touch" before your dog touches the target stick.

Once your dog knows "Touch," you can begin to differentiate between touching the target stick with his nose ("Nose it") and touching it with his paw ("Paw it"). Make it easy for your dog by putting the target stick close to either his nose or his paw. Wait for him to touch it appropriately before you click and treat. If you're working on "Paw it," click and treat each time he does. As he gets "Paw it," move the stick around so he has to work a bit to touch it with his paw.

You can teach "Nose it" as well. Teach this the same way you taught "Paw it," only click and treat when he noses the target stick.

Tip

Many training facilities and even pet supply stores sell clickers and target sticks, but you can also purchase them online from Karen Pryor's website at www.clickertraining.com or by calling 1-800-47-CLICK (1-800-472-5425). If you want to make your own target stick, buy a yard-long half-inch dowel and either paint it or wrap it with colorful tape.

Walking on Leash

Walking on leash is a skill every well-behaved dog needs to know. If your dog has never been on a leash before, put a training collar on him and clip the leash to the training collar.

At first, he may whirl around you or start pulling. Ignore the bad behavior and just wait. When he no longer pulls, click and treat. You'll have to be patient with him and wait for him to stop pulling before you treat. Continue to click and treat for a loose leash.

Once he's waiting for you without pulling, start walking. If he keeps his leash loose, click and treat. If he starts pulling on the leash, stop and wait. When he gives you the loose leash, click and treat. Whenever he pulls, stop immediately and wait for him to give you a loose leash. Then, click, treat, and start on your way again.

Your dog will soon figure out that walking with a loose leash means going forward and more clicks, and that pulling means nothing fun is happening. Because walking is a reward in itself, once he has learned the loose-leash concept, you can *fade* the clicker.

Definition

To **fade** is to slowly and gradually remove an intermediate training object, such as a clicker or target stick, or an intermediate cue to leave the end result—the cue and the action.

The Five Basic Commands

Every dog should know five basic commands for good behavior: "Sit," "Down," "Stay," "Come," and "Heel." In this section, you'll learn how to use the clicker to teach these basic commands.

Sit

To teach "Sit," you'll need to hold a treat or the target stick just above your dog's nose. Tell your dog to "Nose it," and bring the treat or target stick back over his head, toward his tail. As he follows the treat or the target stick, his rump will start to drop. When it touches the floor, click and treat. Repeat several times.

Some dogs might not naturally sit. If your dog won't sit or if he backs up instead of sitting, try teaching him with his back to the wall so he must sit because he doesn't have anywhere to go.

Once you have your dog sitting with the clicker, add the cue word. Tell him, "Rusty, sit!" before having him sit with either the treat or the target stick. Once your dog is familiar with the cue, you can fade the lure or target stick and stop telling him to nose it. Instead, substitute it with the cue to sit.

Down

At times, you'll need for your dog to lie down. To teach "Down," hold a treat or the target stick below your dog's nose. Tell your dog to "Nose it," and bring the treat or target stick downward toward his chest and then all the way to the floor. As he follows the treat or the target stick, his front legs will start to drop. When his elbows touch the floor, click and treat. Repeat several times.

Once you have your dog lying down with the clicker, add the cue. Tell him, "Max, down!" before having him lie down with either the treat or the target stick. Once your dog is familiar with the command, you can fade the lure or target stick and stop telling him to nose it. Instead, substitute it with the cue to lie down.

Stay

Stay is another important command for your dog to know. To teach him "Stay," have him sit beside you while on leash. Do not click yet. Tell him "Stay!" and hold up your flat, open hand in front of his face for emphasis. Take a step or two, and turn to face him. If he gets up, put him back in sit and don't click yet. Once you're facing your dog and he's held the sit for a few seconds, click and treat. Return to him, release him with "Okay," and click and treat.

Note that a puppy younger than 6 months old can't be expected to stay longer than a few seconds. There are too many interesting things out there to explore!

Come

You'll need your dog to come to you at some point, whether it's for his dinner or to stop him from running into the street. To teach him "Come," you and your dog must be in an enclosed area. This is very important, because if your dog sees something he'd rather chase or isn't yet reliable, he'll learn that he only has to come when he feels like it. If you're unable to train in an enclosed area, use a retractable leash or a tracking lead. Keep him on the lead or leash until you're back in a secure area.

Let your dog loose in your enclosed area (or have him on a retractable leash). When they know you have the clicker, most dogs will come right to you. If yours does come right to you, click and treat. If he enjoys running loose too much and doesn't want to come to you, try showing him the treat, then click and treat when he comes.

Once he comes to you, start using the cue word "Come!" You can pair it with your dog's name, such as, "Max, come!" and click and treat when he does.

Once your dog comes to you reliably, put a leash on him and put him in a sit-stay. Walk out to the end of his leash. Be careful that he doesn't break his stay in his enthusiasm to come to you. If he does, put him back in his sit-stay. Then, tell him to come again. Click and treat when he comes.

Practice "Come" at short distances. Then, gradually lengthen the distance with a long-line or a retractable leash. When you call your dog in, either retract the leash or quickly reel in the long-line. If at any time your dog fails to come directly to you, return to shorter distances.

Heel

A well-trained dog should know the heel command. When he heels, he should be beside you, on your left side, facing forward. This is known as the heel position and is also the correct position for him to be in when he sits and lies down. When you walk your dog, you should be holding the leash loosely in your left hand to control the dog, with any excess length of leash looped in your right hand. This will give you the maximum control over your dog—even if he's large and strong.

To put your dog in the heel position, have your dog on a leash but let him move about freely. As he approaches your left side, click and treat. He might be surprised by your click and treat, but he will try to repeat the performance. As he does, click and treat and shape the behavior until he is standing at your side. When he stands or sits for a few moments in heel position, click and treat. Use a one-word cue such as "Heel" or "Place." Practice putting your dog in the heel position, and click and treat when he stands or sits straight in that position.

Once your dog knows the heel position, you can teach him to heel. Your dog should be sitting in heel position with his training collar and leash on. Have a treat in your left hand. Say "Max, heel!" and start walking, putting your left foot forward first. If your dog starts to forge ahead or lag behind, get his attention by showing him the treat and luring him into the correct position. Click and treat when he's in the correct position. If he lags because he's unsure of what to do, pat your leg and encourage him to come beside you. If he forges ahead, stop and wait for him to stop pulling and go back to the heel position. When he does, click and treat.

When you stop, have him sit in the heel position, then click and treat. When you start again, always start by moving your left foot forward first. Dogs see your left leg move before they see your right one. This also becomes another signal to your dog that he is to move with you.

High-Tech Training: Does It Work?

Maybe you've seen signs or advertisements for invisible fencing and wonder if it and other high-tech training gadgets really work. Are they effective? Are they harmful to your dog? Let's look at some of them so you can decide for yourself.

Did You Know? _____

Many of the latest training aids, such as invisible fences and no-bark collars, use electric shocks to contain the dog. While they can and do work, these are a form of negative training, which works as punishment for an undesired behavior rather than training the dog right the first time. These shocks can be very unpleasant, and many people consider them cruel.

Invisible Fencing

The concept of "invisible fences" or electronic fencing is pretty simple: a charged, sometimes buried boundary wire (or a post) emits a frequency that's picked up by an electronic collar worn by the dog. When the dog gets close to the boundary, he receives a shock or a series of shocks (or, in the case of some more humane versions, an audible tone). The dog learns to avoid the boundary and stays inside.

That's the theory; the reality is a little more complex. You have to train your dog to learn the boundaries and to understand how the invisible fence works so he doesn't simply get shocked and can't figure out why. You can't just turn him loose and expect it to work. And a really determined dog (or a dog who sees something worth chasing) will brave the shock and clear the fence, free to run about. You also have to remember that the collar batteries can die and the dog might find he can go outside the yard with no shock. Also, an invisible fence may keep your dog in, but it won't keep other dogs or people out.

Depending on the type of fence, your dog usually receives a shock only when he crosses the boundary (in or out).

Warning _____

One problem with invisible fences is that once the dog crosses the boundary, if he tries to re-enter your yard, he'll get shocked again.

You might also find sonic fences, but these really don't provide enough of deterrent to consider effective.

Are these a good alternative to fences? No. They won't keep your dog safe and in many cases can cause behavior problems like aggression. These may only be useful if there is no other alternative available.

No-Bark Collars

If your designer dog is a barker, you might be tempted to try a no-bark collar. There are three types of no-bark collars: sonic, electric shock, and citronella. Of the three, the most effective and humane collar is the citronella collar.

A citronella no-bark collar is an alternative to a standard no-bark collar. When the dog barks, the collar sprays a fine mist of citronella on the dog's chin. Most dogs dislike the smell and quickly learn to be quiet to avoid the citronella. However, some dogs are clever enough to turn their head to avoid the mist, or will quickly bark several times to empty the canister.

Only use a citronella collar if your dog is noisy when you're not at home.

If he's barking when you're home, in most cases it's his way of expressing boredom. If he barks when he's bored, it's become a habit for him. Once started, it's hard to stop. To stop your dog from barking, try the following instead:

- Keep your dog inside at night and during the day when you're not home.

- Use the pennies-in-a-pop-can trick: place 5 to 10 pennies in several pop cans, then tape the top so the pennies stay inside and rattle when you shake the can. When you catch your dog doing something bad, throw a can in your dog's direction—but *don't hit him!*—close enough to startle him and interrupt his barking.

🏠 Fill a squirt bottle with clean water (you can also use one of those big soaker water guns). When you catch your dog barking, squirt him—but stay away from his face (you want to interrupt his barking, not hurt his eyes). Most dogs don't like being squirted and will soon stop.

🏠 Spend extra time with your dog, exercising, training, and playing with him. This will not only cure his boredom, but will help you two bond.

Electronic Static Mats

If your dog is constantly getting into places he shouldn't, such as cruising the counters or lying on the sofa, one technological innovation is the electric static mat. These mats produce a low-level correction shock that feels exactly like a static shock—unpleasant, but not painful. Most dogs avoid the mats to the point that you can leave them turned off and the dogs will still avoid them.

Dog Toys!

Dogs, like people, need some fun. Most dogs need chews and other toys to satisfy their excessive energy. It's tough finding the right dog toys, though, because most are made to tear apart easily and your dog won't want to touch the ones that are virtually indestructible.

Here are some suggestions for good entertainment for your dog:

🏠 **Bones, rawhide, and other chews.** These chews are perhaps the most enticing, but an aggressive chewer can make short work of these, so it's important to watch your dog while he chews them, and take the chew away if he tears off large portions that can be swallowed. Small bones such as chicken, turkey, pork chops, or steak bones can perforate an intestine and can cause a blockage. If you give your dog bones, give him thick marrow-bones or knuckle bones that are hard to break off into pieces.

- 🏠 **Nylon bones.** Nylon bones tend to be less dangerous than regular bones, but your dog can still snap pieces off and swallow them if your dog is an aggressive chewer or if the size is wrong for your dog. Try Nylabone brand (www.nylabone.com).

- 🏠 **Hard rubber toys.** These are usually safe, provided you get a toy large enough for your dog. But dogs can and do chew up nearly indestructible toys, so monitor him with all toys. One company well known for hard rubber toys is Kong (www.kongcompany.com).

- 🏠 **Fleece and fabric toys.** Most dogs love these toys; however, they can be pulled apart and chewed up. When giving your dog a fleece toy, watch him carefully when he has it and remove it when you're unable to watch him.

> **Warning**
>
> It's important to watch your dog's chewing habits and to realize that no toy is 100 percent indestructible or safe. Always watch your dog when he chews or plays with a toy, and take away any toy your dog tears apart or chews into portions he can swallow. Toys that can be ripped apart or chewed into bits may cause an obstruction in your dog's intestines, which can be costly to remove or even fatal.

Some of the latest training aids include high-tech dog toys. These toys are intended to be interactive with your dog and provide mental stimulation as well as hours of play:

- 🏠 **Buster Cube.** This is a plastic food cube puzzle, with different levels of difficulty. You fill all the Buster Cube's compartments with food and show your dog that by pushing the cube around with his nose in certain ways, he can get a treat (www.bustercube.com).

🐾 **Crazy Ball**. This works on a similar principle as the Buster Cube: the dog must push the ball around to get the treats (www.nylabone.com).

🐾 **Talk to Me Treatball.** This toy enables you to record a 15-second message for your dog, and it activates and dispenses a treat when he rolls the treatball (www.talktometreatball.com).

The Least You Need to Know

🐾 Using a crate will help your dog housetrain more quickly.

🐾 Never leave a puppy in a crate longer than 4 hours.

🐾 The basic commands your dog should know are sit, down, stay, heel, and come.

🐾 Electronic aids are only as good as the training.

🐾 No toys are 100 percent safe. Watch your dog carefully until you learn his chewing habits.

Health and Your Designer Dog

In This Chapter

- 🏠 Understanding what congenital and hereditary diseases affect your designer dog
- 🏠 Choosing the right veterinarian for your designer dog
- 🏠 Looking at pet health insurance

After you, your vet is your dog's best friend. Together, the two of you work to ensure his health and happiness. In this chapter, you'll learn how to find the best veterinarian for your designer dog. You'll learn the most common hereditary diseases found in designer dogs and also if pet health insurance is a good idea.

Choosing a Veterinarian

Your dog's veterinarian is one of the most important people in his life. The vet can offer guidance on how to care for your dog and what to do when he's sick. It only makes sense that you find the right vet for your dog.

When you look for a vet, he or she should be compatible with you. This might sound strange, but whether or not you get along with your vet will affect whether you're willing to follow his or her directions.

You can afford to be a bit picky when choosing a vet. Although most vets offer similar services, not all vets offer the same services. For example, some vets offer mobile services (they come to you); others offer emergency services, boarding, grooming, or other specialized care. When looking for a vet, consider what services you're looking for. Price shouldn't be the only consideration.

Where Vets Work

Veterinarians work at a variety of facilities, including ...

- **Veterinary clinics.** Vet clinics may have as few as one or as many as five or more vets. These clinics have office hours and may or may not handle emergencies.

- **Animal hospitals.** These hospitals usually employ a large number of vets and may have specialists as well. They might have their own testing facilities that a smaller clinic can't afford. They may handle complex surgeries and emergencies that can't be treated anywhere else.

- **Emergency clinics.** These vet clinics are for emergencies only. These clinics usually handle after-hours calls and tend to be expensive.

- **Low-cost clinics.** A relatively new type of vet clinic, the purpose behind most low-cost clinics is to provide routine services (vaccinations, heartworm tests, spay/neuters, etc.) at a low cost. These clinics make up in volume for their lower prices. They generally don't have the facilities to handle emergencies or complex diagnoses.

- **Mobile clinics.** Usually a limited clinic, mobile clinics are commonly associated with an animal hospital or a veterinary clinic. They offer convenience to the pet owner.

- **University clinics.** These clinics are usually state of the art when it comes to treating pets with unusual conditions or serious diseases such as cancer.

Locating a Vet

Finding the best dog doc in your neighborhood might be just a call away. Ask your dog-owning friends and neighbors who their vet is. A glowing recommendation is worth its weight in gold—the good vets don't need to advertise. Most get their clients through word of mouth.

But what if you can't find any good recommendations? Try contacting your dog's breeder to see if she has suggestions. Even if the breeder doesn't live in your area, she can ask other breeders in your area whom they take their dogs to. Try trainers and groomers in your area, too. They might be able to recommend someone.

> **Tip**
> If you're stuck, you can contact the American Animal Hospital Association (AAHA) for a list of vets in your area. Find the AAHA online at www. aahanet.org/, or contact them at PO Box 150899, Denver, CO 80215-0899; 303-986-2800.

You can also look through the Yellow Pages under veterinarians and make a list of vets in your area. With your list in hand, call the vets and ask questions such as the following:

- What is the cost for vaccinations, office visits, and other routine services?

- What hours is your clinic open? Do you offer after-hours services?

- Do you handle emergencies, or are you affiliated with a clinic that handles emergencies? Are the vets on call and do they have an on-call pager?

- Do any of the vets specialize in a particular area such as allergies, neurology, or holistic treatments?

- Do you offer on-site grooming or boarding?

- Do you offer a multi-pet discount?

- Do you take pet insurance?

- Do you make house calls? Under what circumstances?

- How many designer dogs like mine do you see?

The staff at the clinic should be courteous and willing to answer your questions. And keep in mind that there are no right or wrong answers to these questions. The questions are to help you narrow down your choices for a veterinarian.

Once you've narrowed down the vets to a few choices, call each vet and schedule an appointment to visit the facility. Don't drop by unannounced—you might show up during a busy time when the staff may not have a chance to talk with you. When you do visit, ask for a tour. The clinic should be clean, and the staff should be

> **Tip**
>
> A good time to visit the veterinarian is usually Tuesdays or Wednesdays in the morning or afternoon, when fewer people make appointments.

friendly and helpful. If you have a chance to talk with the vet, do so. Find out what the vet's training is and if he or she is familiar with conditions common to your designer dog. If you're interested in holistic medicine, find out if the veterinarian uses holistic therapies or is strictly a conventional vet.

You should have a good feeling about the veterinarian and the clinic before you decide to bring your dog there. The final test is usually when you bring in your dog for his first appointment. Although some dogs won't get along with any vet, the vet should have a gentle and caring manner toward your dog.

Protecting Your Designer Dog's Health

Veterinary costs can be expensive, especially in the first year of your dog's life. However, you must care for your designer dog with routine medical exams, vaccinations, and dewormings, or risk having a sick dog or worse. Remember, the purchase price of a dog doesn't include health care, training, or food.

Did You Know? _____

It might be little consolation to know that veterinary care is a bargain when compared to human medical costs and that with the same procedures performed on dogs and humans, the human treatment is hundreds or even thousands of dollars more than what a vet charges.

Vets have to pay for their practice; pay their staff; pay for their education, equipment, supplies, and other things; plus still feed a family and invest in their business. They price procedures at levels that they can reasonably expect their clientele to pay (hence, the wide range in price).

Veterinary Costs

When you purchase a dog, you can expect some set health-care costs the first year. The following is an estimate, and the cost depends on the area you live in, your dog's health, and the cost the vet charges. Some veterinarians may charge more or less, and if your dog has health problems, the cost may go up substantially.

Service (and Frequency)	Cost/Service	Total Cost
Office visits (5)	$15 to $30	$75 to $150
Vaccinations (4; 3 combo and rabies)	$10 to $50	$40 to $200
Lyme vaccine (2)	$20 to $75	$40 to $150
Bordetella (2)	$25 to $50	$50 to $100
Fecal exam (1)	$25 to $50	$25 to $50
Dewormings (2)	$20 to $50	$40 to $100
Spay/neuter (1)	$50 to $200	$50 to $200
Heartworm test (1)	$20 to $70	$20 to $70
Heartworm preventive (2)	$25 to $50	$50 to $100
Totals		**$390 to $1,120**

After the first year, you'll have ongoing maintenance such as yearly vaccinations, dewormings, and heartworm and flea prevention, plus costs any time your dog gets sick. The cost creeps back up after about 8 years of age, when your dog starts settling into middle age and old age.

The cost of vaccinations largely depends on whether your dog is at risk of contracting certain diseases and whether your vet thinks it's important for your dog to have these vaccinations. Certain vaccinations against deadly diseases such as *distemper, parvovirus,* and rabies are necessary even in adults, but other vaccinations such as *Lyme disease, Giardia,* or *Bordetella* are strictly dependent on whether your dog has a high risk of exposure to these diseases.

Definition

Distemper is a virus that is nearly always fatal in dogs. It affects the nervous system and occasionally the gastric system and is spread through the air and through contact. **Parvovirus** is a virus that kills 50 percent of puppies. It attacks the gastric system. **Lyme disease** is a bacteria that's spread through ticks and the blood of infected dogs. **Bordetella** is a bacteria that causes kennel cough. It's spread through the air. **Giardia** is a single-cell organism that causes diarrhea and gastric distress. It's contracted through contaminated water.

Pet Health Insurance

Even on the low end, that's a fair amount of money. Luckily, you can get pet health insurance to help with some vet costs, and it's available for your designer dog. Some insurance plans cover only major medical expenses, while others take care of routine health care.

Although price is important, it's also important to know that the insurance comes from a reputable source, has been around for a long time, and won't disappear tomorrow. Read the policy information carefully—some only cover catastrophic injuries or diseases (like a major medical) and some are like an HMO or PPO. The more routine services covered, the more expensive the insurance is likely to be.

Tip

See Appendix B for a list of pet health insurance companies.

When checking out the insurance, be sure to get the AM Best rating, that is, an insurance rating that tells you how good the insurance is and how reliable the underwriter of the policy is. Typically, most experts recommend an A+ or A++ rating (the higher the rating, the more confidence you should have in the insurance).

Most pet health insurance won't cover preexisting conditions, elective surgery, or hereditary diseases. Many also have a cap on diseases such as cancer. Most insurance becomes more expensive over time, so it's best to buy it when your dog is a puppy.

Is it a good value? This depends largely on if you need to use it. Many pet owners who would normally have to put their pets down because of an expensive illness have the option of treating the disease instead. Usually the owner must pay for the procedure and then get reimbursed by the health insurance.

Warning

Pet health insurances come and go, so be very careful in your selection. You don't want to have paid hundreds of dollars each year, only to have the insurance company disappear when your dog is in the emergency room.

Hereditary Diseases and the Designer Dog

As long as there are genes, there will be genetic diseases. Although reputable breeders go to great lengths to eradicate genetic diseases in their lines, other breeders, puppy mills, and backyard breeders are breeding dogs haphazardly and perpetuating poor health.

Some genetic diseases can be successfully screened for. For example, reputable breeders have screened for hip dysplasia, effectively reducing or eliminating the numbers of dysplastic dogs in their lines. However, in many circumstances, there is no reliable test for certain genetic diseases and a disease will crop up after the breeder thought she had eradicated it.

The designer dog suffers from genetic diseases just like his purebred counterparts. These diseases affect all dogs—not just purebreds.

Allergies

You might be surprised to hear that dogs have allergies, too. Dogs suffer from an extraordinary number of allergies; some are severe, some not so. Most allergies are hereditary. Your dog can suffer from certain external (contact) exposure and also from allergy to food.

Some contact allergies are apparent, but some aren't as easy to diagnose. For example, if your dog's skin looks irritated and is itchy after you wash him with a particular shampoo, you might guess that your dog is allergic to a chemical in that shampoo. However, you might not know why your dog's nose and face are swollen and irritated. Many dogs are allergic to plastic or rubber and may react to their plastic food bowls. Most contact allergy diagnoses are based on the owner's observations.

Food allergies usually manifest themselves as skin or stomach disorders. Dogs can be allergic to certain ingredients in their food such as corn or wheat, or the protein source, such as beef, soy, or lamb. These types of allergies manifest themselves with digestive upsets and skin problems.

Dietary allergies are a bit tricky to diagnose. Your vet will recommend a hypoallergenic diet for several weeks. This diet usually has a novel protein source—that is, a protein source that dogs generally don't eat, such as fish, venison, or even kangaroo meat. It might have an unusual carbohydrate source, too, such as potatoes. After your dog is on this diet several weeks, you add the potential problem ingredients one at a time to determine what the allergy is. Some dog owners are so relieved to have their dogs allergy free that they keep them on the hypoallergenic diet.

Flea allergy dermatitis is another allergy that many dogs have. It can be eliminated by eliminating the fleas.

Other allergies are trickier to diagnose. You might have to have your vet screen your dog for possible allergens and go from there.

Elbow Dysplasia and Osteochondritis Dissecans

Elbow dysplasia (ED) is a hereditary disease that causes the elbow joints to be malformed. This disease is called *polygenic* because several genes may cause it.

Surgery, anti-inflammatories, and *nutriceuticals* are recommended treatments for ED. Obviously, surgery can be very expensive, and arthritis often sets in to the joints, further complicating matters. You should never breed a dog with elbow dysplasia.

Osteochondrosis dissecans (OCD) is a condition causing the cartilage in the joints to thicken. This thickened cartilage is more prone to damage and may tear and form a flap or rejoin to the bone, which requires surgery to remove. OCD may appear in

Definition

A trait or condition coming from more than one gene pair is **polygenic**. A **nutriceutical** is a nutritional supplement intended to help mitigate a condition or disease.

several joints or in only one. OCD can be very painful, and if your dog has this condition, he may become limp after exercising, suggesting that perhaps this is an injury. You might feel the joint pop or crackle as you examine it. OCD's onset is usually between 4 and 8 months of age, and it will cause persistent lameness if left untreated. If your dog is diagnosed with OCD, your veterinarian may recommend that you rest your dog for several weeks.

Although OCD can be due to trauma, when it is paired with elbow dysplasia, it is most likely due to hereditary conditions.

Epilepsy

Epilepsy exists in all breeds and mixed breeds. It is usually hereditary in dogs and can be quite prevalent in some lines. Studies show some breeds have a genetic predisposition to epilepsy. "Idiopathic" epilepsy (epilepsy where the specific cause is not known) in dogs is very similar to epilepsy in humans. However, other causes of epilepsy must be ruled out before declaring the condition to be idiopathic, including trauma to the head, poisoning, tick paralysis, parasites, certain vitamin deficiencies, overheating, intestinal obstructions, liver problems, and calcium imbalances.

If your dog is epileptic, your vet will need to perform some tests to determine or rule out a cause. If the seizures are frequent or become worse, your vet usually will prescribe a medication to help control them. You should never breed a dog with epilepsy.

Warning

Rage syndrome, often called "Springer rage," is a type of seizure during which the dog becomes suddenly aggressive and bites for no reason. It's called Springer rage because it often appears in Springer Spaniels, but it can appear in any dog. Dogs who have Rage syndrome are dangerous, and there is no cure.

Eye Disease

Dogs are prone to a variety of hereditary and congenital eye diseases, many of which can lead to blindness:

- **Cataracts** are cloudiness of the eye's lens. The lens may develop a small dot or become opaque, causing complete blindness. Cataracts can be due to either hereditary or environmental reasons. Juvenile cataracts are usually hereditary but dogs may have adult cataracts later in life.

- **Entropion** is a hereditary condition in which the eyelid turns inward into the eye, causing the eyelashes and fur to rub against the eyeball. It is obviously irritating to the dog and usually requires surgery to correct.

- **Ectropion** is a condition in which the lower eyelid droops, exposing its interior. In mild cases, your veterinarian might prescribe eye drops, an antibiotic, and corticosteroid ophthalmic ointment. In severe cases, surgery may be required.

- **Glaucoma** is a condition in which the body overproduces fluid inside the eyeball and builds up intense pressure. Some forms of glaucoma are due to injury and other conditions, but some forms are inherited. Glaucoma usually requires surgical removal of the entire eye.

- **Hermeralopia** is a hereditary eye condition in which the dog can see well at night, but is blind in daytime or "normal" light conditions. Dogs who suffer from hermeralopia frequently stumble and run into things during the daytime, but have no problem seeing and getting around in low-light conditions.

Did You Know?

A dog's eyesight is typically 20/50. Some Sighthounds and other breeds have better vision; others have worse.

🏠 **Progressive retinal atrophy (PRA)** and **central progressive retinal atrophy (CPRA)** are two degenerative eye disorders that lead to blindness.

A veterinary ophthalmologist can determine whether your dog has these or other eye diseases.

Luxating Patella

Luxating patella is a condition in which the knee slips out of place. Often called "slipped stifle," this can be a painful condition and can only be corrected through surgery. It is either a hereditary or congenital condition.

Zinc-Responsive Dermatosis

With zinc-responsive dermatosis, the dog's body fails to absorb enough zinc from the dog's food, even if the diet has adequate amounts. Symptoms include scaly nose, paw pads, and belly. It may be confused with pemphigus, or "Collie nose." Treatment of zinc-responsive dermatosis requires additional zinc supplementation to the dog's diet. This disease usually has a genetic component and is more common in Nordic breeds and their mixes. Dogs displaying clear signs of zinc-responsive dermatosis should not be bred.

Protein-Losing Necropathy and Protein-Losing Enteropathy

Protein-losing necropathy (PLN) and protein-losing enteropathy (PLE) are conditions in which either the intestines or the kidneys are unable to process protein correctly and actually lose protein. PLE/PLN can occur anytime within the dog's life and cannot be reliably screened for until the clinical signs are present. PLE/PLN is a genetic disease, but because the mode of inheritance is unknown, it may have an environmental component. Dogs with PLE or PLN will lose weight, show food allergies, and have diarrhea and vomiting. Veterinarians can diagnose PLE or PLN with a blood chemistry and urine test.

Von Willebrand's Disease

Von Willebrand's disease (vWD) is a blood-clotting disorder. Some dogs are more severely affected than others. Von Willebrand's disease exists in both inherited and acquired forms. The acquired form is associated with familial autoimmune thyroid disease. Your veterinarian can diagnose vWD through a blood test.

Dogs with vWD are more susceptible to uncontrollable bleeding. If your dog has vWD, your veterinarian should take precautions during surgery to avoid having the dog bleed out. Likewise, you should take precautions to avoid the chance of injuring your dog if he has vWD.

Hip Dysplasia

Hip dysplasia (HD) is a crippling genetic disease caused by the malformation of the hip socket. No amount of good nutrition and care will stop it, but in mild cases, your vet may be able to help mitigate the effects with nutriceuticals such as glucosamine, chondroitin, and creatine, and anti-inflammatories such as aspirin. Some cases are so bad that the dog must have surgery. In some extreme cases, the dog must be euthanized.

Surgery is extremely expensive, costing thousands of dollars in most cases, which is why it's very important to purchase your purebred from a reputable breeder. You should never breed a dog with hip dysplasia or without an Orthopedic Foundation for Animals (OFA) or PennHIP rating of *Good* or *Excellent* hips.

Legg-Calve-Perthes Disease

Legg-Calve-Perthes disease is a crippling genetic hip disease. Found in many small dogs and toy breeds, the blood supply to the femoral head in the leg bone is cut off and causes the bone cells to die. At some point, the blood supply is reestablished and the bone tries to rebuild, or it sometimes collapses on itself. In either case, the femoral head becomes malformed and doesn't fit properly in the hip socket.

Surgery is usually the only option with Leggs-Calves-Perthes disease, and because this is likely to be hereditary, you should never breed a dog with hips less than an OFA excellent or good.

Hypothyroidism

Hypothyroidism occurs when the dog's thyroid gland does not produce enough thyroid hormone. Symptoms can include lethargy, a dull and dry coat, obesity or weight gain, and a thinning coat. The dog may seek warmer areas. Hypothyroidism can cause infertility in intact males and females.

Some forms of hypothyroidism may be hereditary, so it is inadvisable to breed a hypothyroid dog. Your vet can diagnose hypothyroidism through a blood test. If your dog is hypothyroid, your veterinarian may prescribe a form of thyroid hormone. OFA has a relatively new thyroid registry. Breeders should test and register their dogs with the OFA.

Heredity Myopathy of Labrador Retrievers

Heredity Myopathy of Labrador Retriever (HMLR) is a muscle disorder found only in Labrador Retrievers and their mixes in which the dog has a marked deficiency of muscle mass due to a deficiency of a type of muscle fiber. The condition starts showing signs when the puppy is 3 or 4 months old. The puppy may be weak and have a stiff, hopping gait. He may collapse after what would be considered normal exercise.

Cold weather and stress may aggravate symptoms and cause collapse. The severity of the condition varies and usually stabilizes by the time the puppy is 6 months to 1 year. Obviously puppies with this condition can't work, although they can be pets. Further studies are being done on this disease, and a blood test to detect carriers of this disease might soon be available.

Aortic Stenosis and Subvalvular Aortic Stenosis

Aortic Stenosis (AS) and Subvalvular Aortic Stenosis (SAS) are insidious hereditary heart conditions that may show no outward sign in an apparently healthy dog. Then, suddenly the dog may simply drop over dead. AS and SAS are caused by a narrowing of the outflow tract of the left ventricle, below the aortic valve. The heart must work harder to push blood through the narrow opening, causing more problems.

SAS can be difficult to diagnose. A heart murmur, a common symptom of SAS, may be difficult to detect. The dog may also have arrhythmias. A veterinary cardiologist can diagnose SAS through either a Doppler echocardiography or cardiac catheterization. The prognosis for a long, healthy life is poor.

Tricuspid Valve Dysplasia

Tricuspid valve dysplasia (TVD) is a hereditary heart condition. With TVD, the tricuspid valve in the heart is deformed, causing the valve not to close tightly. Blood leaks from the valve into the right atrium of the heart, causing the right side of the heart to enlarge. TVD can be mild to severe. Puppies with mild TVD can live somewhat normal lives, but puppies with severe TVD will die before they reach a year.

The Least You Need to Know

- Next to you, your veterinarian is the most important person in your dog's life, overseeing his health. Choose your vet according to his or her specialty and the services you need.

- The cost of veterinary care covers the cost of the veterinary practice, the staff's salaries, equipment, and other factors.

- Veterinary health insurance can help defray the cost of high veterinary bills.

- Designer dogs are susceptible to both hereditary and congenital conditions.

Safety and Identification

In This Chapter

🏠 Protecting your designer dog

🏠 Finding your designer dog if he's lost or stolen

🏠 Understanding high-tech (and low-tech) identification

No one wants to lose a pet, but it can and does happen. Knowing how to keep your designer dog safe is the first step, and having proper identification on your dog is important, too. But what do you do if your designer dog has been dog-napped? Or if he's lost or stolen? In this chapter, I address safety issues and also discuss the latest identification options.

Keeping Your Designer Dog Safe

One of the worries every conscientious dog owner has is how to keep his or her dog safe. Stories abound about gangs of dog thieves—some looking for specific dogs to sell as pets or to breed, to use for dogfights, or to sell to laboratories for research. The prospect of having your dog stolen is frightening, and although the price tag of your designer dog might mean little to you, it might mean something to a dog thief.

But let's be honest. Most dogs who are missing usually get out of the house by accident: someone left a gate open, the dog slipped by you when you opened the door, the dog dug under the fence and got out. There are plenty of innocent reasons why your dog got out.

If you have a yard, it should be fenced so your designer dog can be contained safely. The fence should be tall enough that your dog can't jump over it, and should be built so he won't dig under it if he's a digger. The gate latch should be secure and shouldn't be able to be opened by a clever pooch. (Yes, dogs can and do figure out how to open simple latches!) Never expect your dog to stay in your yard without some type of containment system—even the best-behaved dogs wander when there's something interesting out there.

Did You Know?

The USDA Animal Care Office sponsors a website for missing pets where you can post your missing pet for free: www.missingpet.net.

Protecting Your Designer Dog from Thieves

But having a secure yard only goes so far. Even if your dog's secure in the yard, thieves could still grab him. The truth is, if a really clever thief wants your dog, short of keeping your dog inside 24/7, he's going to steal your dog. However, you can take some precautions to reduce the risk:

- Don't advertise to the world that you have a designer dog. When strangers ask what kind of dog you have, tell them he's a mutt or a crossbreed. It's better that people think you have a mutt rather than a dog that cost you thousands of dollars.

- Limit access to your home. Do you have workers going through the house all the time? An au pair? A dog-sitter? If so, be sure the people in your house are trustworthy and are bonded and insured.

- 🏠 Don't leave your designer dog outside when you're not home or at night. Most dog-nappings occur when the dogs are left alone in a backyard.

- 🏠 Invest in a good security system for your home.

- 🏠 Microchip your dog (more on this later in this chapter).

If Your Designer Dog Is Lost or Stolen

Let's say your designer dog gets out or perhaps someone has broken into his kennel and taken him. What do you do? Hours count when it comes to a missing dog. Here are some practical steps for locating a missing dog:

- 🏠 Keep a recent photo of your dog handy, and make flyers and signs advertising your missing dog. Rather than putting a name like "Labradoodle" or "Cockapoo" on the flyer, use "Labrador Retriever and Poodle mix." Many people don't know what a "Labradoodle" is.

- 🏠 Go door to door in your neighborhood and ask your neighbors if they have seen your dog. If your dog is lost, perhaps one of them might have seen him roaming around—or better yet, picked him up.

- 🏠 Contact local animal shelters and humane societies and give them a description of your dog. Sometimes they don't have a listing of dogs who have just arrived, or may have them misidentified. Visit the shelters frequently.

- 🏠 If your dog is stolen, report the theft to the police immediately.

- 🏠 Contact the veterinarians in your area. Lost dogs are often brought to vets.

- 🏠 Put a "Lost Dog" ad in your local newspaper. Offer a reward, but don't pay until you see your dog.

🏠 Scour "Found" ads, and don't discount that your dog might be several miles away. Dogs can travel great distances in a very short amount of time.

🏠 Don't give up. Although you have a better chance of recovering your dog within the first few hours after he goes missing, you might still be able to recover him days or even weeks afterward.

Warning

Be very cautious if someone calls you, saying he or she has found your dog and wants money to ship the dog back to you. Scam artists such as this will prey on your desperation and take your money. If someone contacts you regarding your dog, ask that the person bring your dog to a veterinarian or shelter *of your choosing* and have them leave their name and address for the reward. Then you pay the veterinarian or shelter to arrange transport of your dog.

Identification for Your Designer Dog

All dogs should have two forms of ID: permanent (microchip or tattoo) and tags. Permanent ID is important in case your dog's collar and tags are missing, both for locating you and for proving that your dog is indeed *your* dog.

The Lowdown on Microchips

Microchips are a relatively recent form of permanent identification. The microchip is implanted in your dog, between his shoulder blades. It is about the size of a grain of rice and is encased in sterile glass. The chip takes seconds to implant, and is good for life. The microchip is read by holding a scanner over the area. The scanner reads the code on the chip, and the person scanning it must then match the code with a database. The microchip number and your contact information must be registered with a national database.

If you move, you'll have to update the national registry with your new address.

The downside to microchips is that there's no single standard for the technology. Different microchip brands require different scanners, and although some scanners can read more than one microchip, some can't. You also must have a microchip scanner to be able to read the microchip—most people don't have one and aren't aware that microchip technology exists. Most shelters and veterinarians do have scanners that read multiple chips, but there are still a few nonstandard microchips out there. And microchips can be a bit pricey. The cost of the chip and registration fees can be $50 or more.

Did You Know?
You may have heard that microchips can move around or travel from the implant site. Older kinds of microchips did travel, but the new ones have been redesigned so they stay put.

If you want to microchip your dog, find a common microchip such as Avid or Home Again that's recognized in shelters and veterinarian offices. Talk with your veterinarian to find out what chips he or she recommends—and what recovery service he or she suggests.

Tattoos

Tattoos are the low-tech but still effective version of permanent identification. Tattoos should be given by a professional pet tattooist (yes, they really exist). A good pet tattooist will only give a dog a tattoo on the inside of the thigh because it's harder to remove than an ear tattoo (dog thieves will cut an ear off to remove the tattoo).

Like microchips, you need to look to see that a tattoo exists. (Most people don't make a habit of looking beneath a dog's belly, and many don't know about tattoos.) And if your dog is really furry, his leg fur will cover up his tattoo, making it impossible to see. (You'll have to keep that area shaved.)

You'll have to think up an original number for the tattoo; most people use their Social Security number, but that's not the best choice. If you sell or give away your dog, you'll be giving out your Social Security number as well.

And like microchips, the dog's tattoo has to be registered in a database to make it effective. If you don't register it, there's no way to track you if your lost dog—and his tattoo—are found.

Did You Know? _____

You can register a tattooed or microchipped pet with several animal registries (see Appendix B for complete contact information):

- 🏠 AKC Companion Animal Recovery (www.akccar.org)

- 🏠 National Dog Registry (www.natldogregistry.com)

- 🏠 Tattoo-a-Pet (www.tattoo-a-pet.com)

Tags

If you don't have a tag on your designer dog, put one on now! Anyone at a shelter can tell you about a dog who appeared at their shelter with a collar and no tags—and no means of identifying the dog.

There's really no excuse for your dog to have no tags, or to have tags so old that they're unreadable. Tags are cheap and easy to get. Some Internet pet-supply sites offer tags for free, and most pet-supply stores have tag machines that will engrave a tag with whatever you like on them. They cost around $4 to $6 unless you get the gold-plated variety. Put your name, address, and phone number on the tag. It's not a bad idea to have your dog's name on it, too.

Keep all information on the tag up-to-date. If you move or if you're traveling, purchase a tag with that information and the traveling dates listed. And periodically inspect the tag for wear. If it's illegible, get a new one, and get it on your dog's collar.

GPS Locator Collars

The latest in pet recovery is the global positioning system (GPS) collar. If your dog is wearing a GPS collar and gets out of the yard, the collar will alert you via your cell phone and give you your dog's coordinates within a certain area.

Of course, this system is only useful if the dog is wearing his collar; otherwise, the system is useless. Several companies offer these systems. Most are pricey (more than $500) and require a monthly monitoring fee.

It's a scary thought to think of your designer dog getting lost or being stolen, but with a few preventative safety and identification measures, you stand a better chance of finding your dog should something happen to him.

The Least You Need to Know

🏠 Your dog needs to have a permanent form of ID, whether a microchip or a tattoo, and tags.

🏠 If you microchip or tattoo your dog, be sure to register him with a national database. And keep the information current, should you move or change phone numbers.

🏠 If your dog is lost or stolen, minutes count, but don't give up! Dogs have been recovered days or even weeks after they've been missing.

Chapter 16

Should I Breed My Designer Dog?

In This Chapter

- 🏠 Deciding whether you should breed your designer dog

- 🏠 Understanding what it takes to be a reputable breeder

- 🏠 Learning how spaying or neutering is actually healthy for your dog

- 🏠 Knowing what to do if your designer dog is pregnant

Designer dogs are expensive, there's no doubt about it. But should you consider breeding your designer dog to perhaps recoup the cost of your dog? Or were you thinking about breeding your designer dog because you love your dog and want another one just like her? Or maybe you're thinking about creating a new designer breed.

In this chapter, I discuss breeding designer dogs, the truth and the myths behind them, and whether this is something you should do.

Should You Breed Your Designer Dog?

If you read Chapter 4 on reputable breeders, you know that being a breeder isn't a responsibility to be taken lightly. If you bring a puppy into this world, you should be responsible and produce a healthy puppy who someone wants to adopt. You must be willing to do genetic testing and offer health guarantees. You must be willing to take back the dog under any circumstance.

In almost all cases, the answer to the question of whether you should breed your dog is "No, you shouldn't." Here's why:

- It costs a lot of money to do it right. Genetic tests, stud fees, veterinary visits, time off from work, special whelping tools and arrangements, and extra food, all add up quickly. A single breeding without complications could cost you thousands of dollars. One with complications could run even more.

- Many female dogs and puppies die due to complications. Inevitably, about half of all puppies bred by inexperienced people die within the first 8 weeks of life.

- Many poorly bred puppies (designer dogs, purebreds, and mutts) end up in shelters because breeders couldn't sell them.

- Male (and female) dogs can contract an incurable dog venereal disease called brucellosis in the act of breeding. It causes infertility, miscarriages, birth defects, and other problems, and can be passed to the mother and puppies as well. It's even mildly contagious to people.

- There are health benefits associated with spaying and neutering (see the "The Great Spay/Neuter Debate" section later in this chapter).

Breeding Myths

Many people think breeding a dog is a good idea. Some common myths associated with breeding include the following:

🏠 **My female needs to have puppies to "settle her temperament."** Breeding a dog won't change her temperament for the better. She might act maternal while she has the puppies, but not afterward. She might also act aggressive when she has the puppies.

🏠 **My dog will be healthier if she has her first heat.** Your dog will actually be healthier if she's spayed before her first heat. Spaying and neutering is actually healthier for your dog than keeping her intact. See the "Why You Should Spay or Neuter Your Designer Dog" section later in this chapter for some of the health benefits of spaying and neutering.

🏠 **I want to show my kids the miracle of birth.** Don't use your dog as a lesson when you could rent a video and show your kids that instead.

🏠 **My dog is valuable because I paid a lot for him.** The price tag of your dog should reflect the cost the breeder put into the dog. It has nothing to do with the actually value of your dog. Your dog's value comes from what you do with him (training and abilities) and his conformation (not just from bloodlines). If your dog isn't of breeding quality and if you haven't studied what makes a dog breeding quality, you will produce substandard dogs nobody wants.

🏠 **Dogs enjoy sex.** Actually, they don't. It's an instinct, and the act includes a 20-minute to 2-hour (or more) "tie" where the dogs are often in pain and attached.

🏠 **I can recoup the cost of my dog.** Maybe. If everything goes smoothly, if you're able to sell all the dogs you breed, and if there are no complications, you might make some money over what you spent in cost of the breeding, whelping, and caring for the puppies. Remember, this takes 63 days of care plus 56 more days of caring for puppies (and that's not counting health screenings). That's at least 119 days of care for the female and the puppies. Another consideration is the cost of damage a whole litter of puppies will cause. Puppies aren't housebroken,

and they will get into everything by 5 weeks old. You'll be ready to see them go by 8 weeks, guaranteed.

Should You Create a New Designer Breed?

You've bought two different purebreds and decided that the mix would be pleasing to everyone, and think you can create the next designer "breed." Is this something you ought to try?

Plenty of people are doing just this. Whether they hit on the right combination remains to be seen. Whether they're producing dogs of the Labradoodle popularity, or whether they're "barking up the wrong tree," they need to breed responsibly, or they're just adding to the pet overpopulation problem.

Responsible breeding is more than putting two purebreds together to create a crossbreed. Many people who look at these crossbreeds think of them as mutts—they're not about to pay thousands of dollars for a mutt they could find at the local shelter. In fact, plenty of designer breeds are already there—some intentional, some accidental.

The Great Spay/Neuter Debate

You've heard that you should spay or neuter your designer dog. Maybe the breeder or your vet or someone from a shelter or rescue group recommended it, or maybe you signed a contract at adoption or purchase, promising to have your dog altered. Why all the hype about spaying and neutering?

> **Tip**
> If you're serious about breeding your dog, contact a responsible breeder for information on how to do it right. He or she can guide you through the process of getting your dog certified and genetically tested.

Spaying and neutering, that is removing the sex organs from a dog (in a female, removing the uterus and ovaries; in a male, removing the testicles) is a common operation. It prevents a dog from being bred.

Why You Should Spay or Neuter Your Designer Dog

The thought of spaying or neutering a dog just doesn't sit well for some people. But if they took time to look at the benefits of spaying and neutering, they might change their mind:

- Spaying reduces mammary tumors (breast cancer) in female dogs if done before the dog is 2 years old. The earlier you spay, the less chance of breast cancer. If you spay before the first heat cycle, it reduces the chance to less than 1 percent; after the first heat cycle, the risk is about 8 percent. The benefits decrease as the dog gets older, but you will still receive some benefit before the age of 2.

- Spaying eliminates uterine and ovarian cancer in female dogs.

- Neutering reduces anal tumors and possibly prostate cancer in male dogs.

- Neutering eliminates testicular cancer in male dogs.

- Spaying and neutering may help curb certain types of aggression.

- Spaying will eliminate the estrus or heat cycle, which lasts 3 weeks twice a year.

- Spaying and neutering may reduce problem behaviors.

- Spaying eliminates the possibility for pyometra, a life-threatening uterine infection that kills 50 percent of all dogs who get it.

As you can see, spaying and neutering your dog may actually help him or her live longer!

Did You Know? _____

Spaying or neutering usually costs between $50 and $200, depending on the size of the dog, on the complexity of the operation, and on your area. The results are permanent. Many humane societies offer coupons for low-cost spays and neuters. Two organizations, Spay USA and Friends of Animals, offer low-cost spays and neuters (price depending on the region), or they work with veterinarians to help reduce the cost. Contact Spay USA at www.spayusa.org or 1-800-248-SPAY (1-800-248-7729). Contact Friends of Animals at www.friendsofanimals.org or 1-800-321-PETS (1-800-321-7387).

Spaying and Neutering Myths

There are a lot of old wives' tales about spaying and neutering. Let's debunk some of the myths you might have heard:

- **My male dog won't act or look male.** He will, but it might take him a little longer to lift his leg than he would if he was intact. Neutered males also tend to be bigger than their intact counterparts. (And it's a little-known fact that neutered males *can* have sex with females who are in season.)

- **My dog won't guard if he's neutered.** Designer dogs aren't supposed to be guard dogs, nor are they supposed to be aggressive. An aggressive dog is a liability. Neutering doesn't affect the dog's ability to work in the slightest.

- **My dog will become fat and lazy if I neuter him.** Neutering doesn't cause your dog to become fat; overfeeding does. You might have to reduce your dog's food a bit to prevent excess pounds, but that's not a drawback.

- **I can't spay or neuter my dog until he's at least 6 months old.** Actually, you can spay and neuter puppies as young as 8 weeks old. The latest anesthetics have a larger safety factor than those used even 10 or 20 years ago.

What Do I Do If My Dog Is Pregnant?

You meant to get your designer dog spayed. You really did. But she got out of the house once when she was in heat or perhaps you caught her with a stray dog. She's been looking a bit paunchy lately, and you think she's pregnant. What are you going to do? You basically have three options.

Emergency Spays

If you'd been planning on spaying your designer dog, take her to the vet right now and get her spayed. Don't delay. A puppy's full gestation is 63 days, which doesn't leave a lot of time to abort the puppies before they're born. Many vets won't spay a female with puppies near full term.

Mismate Shots

If your designer dog has recently been bred, you can try a mismate shot, which is a shot that aborts the pregnancy with hormones. But this is usually very dangerous and can cause serious problems such as pyometra or anemia. Most vets don't recommend it because of the potential for serious illness or death. Spaying is a much safer and more permanent solution.

Bringing the Puppies to Term—Not Without Risks!

You can have your dog carry her puppies to term, but if you do, realize that there are risks associated with that, as well: you could lose your female dog during

Did You Know?

Plenty of good books are available on breeding and caring for puppies, including *Canine Reproduction* by Phyllis Holst.

whelping. Then, there's a matter of care for both the mom and the pups, which is outside the scope of this book and should be something you consult with your vet about. You're also responsible for finding good homes for the pups.

Of these three options of what to do when your female is pregnant, the safest for the dog is spaying, followed by carrying the puppies to term (which is risky), followed by a mismate shot.

Do consider spaying or neutering your dog, if not for the health benefits, then to reduce the ever-growing pet overpopulation problem.

The Least You Need to Know

- Spaying and neutering has many health benefits, including reducing or eliminating your dog's risk for many types of cancer.

- Breeding dogs is a costly business and shouldn't be entered into lightly.

- If you suspect your dog is pregnant, the safest and most responsible route of action is spaying.

Chapter 17

The Golden Years

In This Chapter

- 🏠 Keeping your dog active and healthy through a long life
- 🏠 Learning how to keep your older designer dog comfortable
- 🏠 Understanding old-age diseases
- 🏠 Deciding if you should get another dog
- 🏠 Coming to terms with euthanasia

Someday you'll notice some graying around your dog's muzzle, or perhaps you'll see that he's a little stiff when he gets up in the morning. Someday you'll wake up and your designer dog will be old.

This isn't a time for sadness; it's a time to enjoy each other. Dogs can and do live healthy and active lives over the age of 10, partly due to genetics, and partly due to medical care, diet, and physical activity. You can't change genetics, but you can make a crucial difference in your designer dog's health and longevity.

How Long Do Designer Dogs Live?

When is a dog *old?* It depends. Just as some people don't seem old even when they're in their 70s, some dogs don't seem old at an age when others do. Good genetics and a lifetime of exercise, good nutrition, and medical care can make the difference between a 10-year-old dog who seems old and one who still acts young.

Many pet books place "seniors" at 7 years or more, but this isn't exactly right. Many dogs, especially those bred from toy breeds, can live to be up to 17 years old with good care. From 8 to 10 years old, you start seeing some changes due to old age. After 10, a dog starts becoming a senior, but he might not quite be a senior until he's much older.

Factors That Affect Your Designer Dog's Life Span

Several factors affect a dog's life span, just as they affect a person's life span. Part of it is genetics, but part of it is also lifestyle, activity level, and general health maintenance.

Breeding

You've probably heard of people who never took care of themselves—were overweight, ate a bad diet, smoked, drank, and behaved dangerously—and lived to 100 years old. Then you hear about the guy who exercises every day, watches his weight and diet carefully, and never touches alcohol or cigarettes—and drops dead at 35 from a massive heart attack.

Doesn't seem fair, does it? But that's how genetics work. We can't change our genetics, but we can be cautious about the genetics we breed in our dogs. A dog who is genetically healthy is more apt to live longer than a dog who is poorly bred to begin with. Plenty of dogs are well cared for but die early because of a ticking genetic time bomb inside them. Responsible breeders can't always foresee the longevity of your dog due to his parents, but you have a better chance at having a healthy, long-lived dog because of it. So by getting a well-bred dog, you've given your dog a chance to live longer.

Care

Genetics is only part of the equation. Even a well-bred dog could die early due to poor care. (He might not get lucky like that guy who lived to 100!) You, as your designer dog's owner, are responsible for his good diet and veterinary care. That means recognizing when your dog is sick and taking him to the vet, and getting appropriate vaccinations, heartworm preventive, dewormings, proper grooming, premium dog food, and good water.

Exercise

The final piece to the longevity puzzle is how much exercise your designer dog gets. Just like people, dogs can easily become obese. Your dog will have a longer and healthier life if he exercises regularly and stays trim.

Did You Know? _____

Exercising can be fun! Your designer dog will enjoy sports such as agility, flyball, and flying disc. Check out my books: *Having Fun with Agility*, *Introduction to Dog Agility*, and *The Simple Guide to Getting Active with Your Dog* (see Appendix C).

Old-Age Ailments

Dogs have more problems when they age, including loss of certain senses, cancers and tumors, and arthritis. Many problems can be mitigated with modern veterinary medicine, but vets aren't miracle workers. If you notice that your dog seems to be slowing down or ailing, it's best to take him to the vet when you notice it, rather than waiting for it to become a bigger problem.

Arthritis

Arthritis seems a constant in older age, both for people and for dogs. If your dog is not active, you might see signs of arthritis early. Some supplements, such as glucosamine and MSM (found in Cosequin, Glycoflex, or Synova-Cre), can help relieve arthritis. These supplements work well on some dogs but do nothing for others. Your dog usually has to be on the supplement for more than 6 weeks before you can see any effect.

Your vet can help mitigate some of the effects of arthritis with anti-inflammatories. Aspirin is a common pain reliever—ask your vet for the proper dosage. Do not give your dog either acetaminophen or ibuprofen—they are very toxic to dogs. Your vet can prescribe the right amount of buffered aspirin, anti-inflammatories, or steroids to alleviate pain and swelling. Keeping your dog off hardwood floors and keeping him warm will go a long way toward making him comfortable.

 Warning

One controversial medication commonly prescribed for arthritis is Rimadyl (also known as Carprofen). Some dogs have contracted liver disease while on Rimadyl. Still, many vets use Rimadyl to help alleviate arthritis pain without problems. If your dog is suffering from arthritis and you want to try Rimadyl, talk to your vet about potential risks and side effects. Your vet might want to run blood tests to determine if your dog is right for Rimadyl.

Other medications within the same family as Rimadyl, such as Zubrin and Dermaxx, might work better or have no effect on your dog's arthritis.

Loss of Senses

Like people, dogs can suffer from loss of hearing and loss of eyesight. You might not even notice it for a while because dogs are very adept at adapting to their disabilities.

If your dog acts as if he's ignoring you, he may be going deaf. Deafness can come on gradually or suddenly. Clap your hands behind your dog's head or rattle the food bowl while he's in the other room. If he doesn't react, he's probably deaf.

If your dog bumps into a new object or runs into objects while on a walk, it's time to visit the vet. Your vet should be able to confirm if your dog is blind.

Once you've determined your dog is blind or deaf, be sure to provide a safe environment for him. Don't rearrange the furniture if you have a blind dog. A deaf dog won't be able to hear you, so you'll have to get his attention visually before you have him do something. Being there and reassuring him will help make him comfortable.

Tip

Your older dog will appreciate a little extra babying during this time of his life. Try the following to make him more comfortable:

- An orthopedic dog bed
- Ramps to get onto the couch and into the car
- Food bowls raised to head height
- Electric heating mats made for dogs
- Softer food

Cognitive Dysfunction Syndrome

Cognitive Dysfunction Syndrome (CDS) is similar to Alzheimer's disease in dogs. This disease shows a marked change in behavior.

Your dog may suddenly look "lost," he may not recognize loved ones, and he may forget his housetraining. His sleep may be disrupted, and he may bark and carry on in the middle of the night.

Brain tumors may mimic CDS, so it's very important to have a brain tumor ruled out first before beginning CDS treatment. CDS treatment of choice is Anipryl, which is also used to treat Cushings disease in dogs. The therapy can be expensive, costing from $50 to $100 a month. Once your dog is on the therapy, he must remain on it his entire life or symptoms will reappear.

Cancer

Cancer and tumors are more prevalent with age. Some cancers and tumors can be eliminated or greatly reduced if you spay or neuter your dog before he or she is 6 months old (see Chapter 16 for more on spaying and neutering).

If you find a new lump or bump on your dog, have it checked immediately. Some cancers and tumors are fast spreading, and if you wait too long, it might be too late for your veterinarian to do anything. Signs of cancer include the following:

- Strange growths
- Excessive weight loss
- Lack of appetite
- Bleeding
- Sores or wounds that do not heal
- Abnormal swellings
- Excessive sleep or lethargy
- Difficulty breathing, eating, or drinking

Treatment for cancer and tumors in dogs is similar to treatment of cancer and tumors in humans, including surgery, chemotherapy, and radiation therapy. Other, newer experimental treatments exist, including gene therapy, but these are mostly untried and very costly.

> **Warning**
>
> Older dogs are more prone to tumors and cancers than younger dogs. Examine your dog for tumors at least once a week, and bring him to the vet if you do find a tumor. Cancer is somewhat difficult to diagnose without running tests. If your dog is eating but losing weight, drinking excessive water, tiring easily, or not eating well at all, take him to the vet for a full examination.

Should You Get Another Dog?

Some people decide to get a puppy as their dog ages to help mitigate the pain of losing the beloved pet when the time finally arrives. This can be good or bad, depending on the circumstances. If your dog is very old, he might look on this new puppy as an interloper. A puppy will take most of your time and energy, leaving little time for your old dog. Your dog might feel neglected and might become aggressive or short-tempered with the new pup.

However, some dogs tolerate puppies well. Sometimes a puppy can spark new life in an old dog, and the new and exciting pup can shake an old dog from the routine enough to make him feel young again. Some older dogs are quick to become the puppy's aunt or uncle, and are delighted to show the newcomer the ropes.

Whether another dog or puppy is accepted largely depends on you and your dog. If your dog gets along with other dogs and puppies, perhaps getting a puppy might be the right choice. At the same time, you must make the time to have your dog feel extra special. Don't stop doing things with her, now that you have the puppy—otherwise she'll associate the lack of attention with the appearance of the "interloper."

Saying Good-Bye

Saying good-bye is perhaps the hardest thing to do as a dog owner. I've had to put several of my dogs down, and the truth is, it doesn't get any easier. Nor is the decision always clear-cut.

Sometimes it's obvious: your dog is in great pain and is dying from a terminal disease or injury. Other times, the diagnosis is unclear, or you're sitting in an emergency room and don't know what to do. Heroic efforts may be required, which cost far beyond what you can afford, and your dog might still have a very slim chance of recovery. In times like this, talk to someone you can trust—perhaps your vet, or another vet for a second opinion. Other dog-owning friends might be able to see clearly when you cannot and offer objective advice.

Don't allow your best friend to suffer needlessly. It's tempting to try heroic actions to save your pet, but you might discover that the end result is still the same. Dogs don't live forever, and even though you want your dog to live a little longer, it might not be humane or even possible.

Euthanasia is quick and painless for your dog. The veterinarian will administer an injection, and your pet will be gone. You can stay with your dog during his final minutes or leave—it's your choice. Many pet owners opt to stay with their dog during the last few minutes, as it comforts the dog and brings closure.

You will grieve. This is normal and natural. Don't talk to non-dog owners who might tell you it was only a pet. No, it wasn't. Your dog was your friend, and it would be callous not to grieve for a good friend who just died. Talk to your vet about your grief. He or she might be able to refer you to free or low-cost pet loss counseling. Many veterinary colleges offer free or low-cost pet loss hotlines.

Most people feel some sort of guilt with the death of their pet. This is normal, too, but you need to be aware that you did everything you could at the time to save your pet. Hindsight is 20/20—don't let yourself be caught up in the guilt of having to put down your dog.

Take care of yourself during this time. Keep busy and active; exercise and eat a balanced diet. Avoid being alone and risking going into depression. You aren't denying that you have grief over the loss—you are helping yourself deal with it.

With time, the pain and anguish of your pet's death will fade. You will start remembering all the good times you had together. Perhaps, in time, you'll be ready to own another designer dog again. Perhaps you will get a puppy to keep you occupied. If you do, remember that no puppy will replace your beloved pet and that no dog will be like your old dog. Your new puppy or dog will have a different personality and different behaviors—do not expect the same thing out of this puppy. In time, you might grow to love this new addition as much as you loved your beloved pet.

> **Tip**
> An excellent pet loss website is www. petloss.com. It has some of the most comprehensive lists of pet loss support groups, hotlines, and information to be found.

The Least You Need to Know

- 🏠 Keeping your older dog active will help him lead a longer, better life.

- 🏠 You old dog will need your help coping with arthritis, blindness, deafness, and other old-age ills.

- 🏠 Carefully consider getting a new puppy as your dog ages.

- 🏠 Don't let your dog suffer needlessly just to postpone the inevitable. Euthanasia can be a very humane thing to do.

- 🏠 You will grieve when your dog dies. That's normal and to be expected. Take care of yourself during this time and remember the good life you had with your dog.

Glossary

alleles   Genes that occupy the same position on the chromosome and govern specific traits, but may be different in how they affect those traits.

autosomal   A gene that is not gender-related.

breed standard   A written description of the ideal dog in a breed. The breed standard is what distinguishes each dog breed from all the others.

conformation show   A type of dog show at which dogs are judged according to how well they conform to the breed standard.

contract   The bill of sale between you and the breeder when you purchase a puppy or dog. It outlines legal obligations such as right of first refusal, spay/neuter clauses, and health guarantees. It protects you, should anything go wrong either with your purchase or with your dog's health, and it gives you legal recourse.

cue   A word or signal your dog learns to associate with a particular behavior.

digestibility   The percentage of nutrients in a dog food that the dog can use after the food is digested.

fade   To slowly remove an intermediate training object, such as a clicker or target stick or an intermediate cue. This leaves the end result—the cue and the action.

genotype   The genetic makeup of the dog.

heterozygous   When two alleles are different. If one is recessive, then it makes the dog a carrier for the recessive trait.

hip dysplasia   A hereditary disease that causes the hip joint to be malformed.

homozygous   When two alleles are the same, or match up.

hybrid   A cross between two species or two varieties within a species.

kill-shelter   A shelter that puts dogs to death after a certain amount of time or when the shelter becomes full.

neoteny   Retaining an immature or puppylike quality into adulthood.

nutriceuticals   A nutritional supplement intended to help mitigate a condition or disease.

open coat   A term used to describe a dog with a single coat or one without an undercoat. These dogs don't shed the same way as double-coated dogs (who frequently shed year-round or twice a year, depending on breed and climate). Dogs with open coats are similar to Poodles and Terriers, and require clipping.

pedigree   A dog's family tree.

performance event   An event at which dogs compete against each other for titles in obedience, agility, tracking, rally, herding, or other types of canine sports.

phenotype   The physical traits you can see in a dog due to the genotype and the environment.

polygenic   A trait or condition caused by more than one gene pair.

progressive retinal atrophy An hereditary disease that leads to blindness in dogs.

puppy mill A place where dogs are produced commercially in which the bottom line is to make money and not to produce a quality dog.

shaping To start with a basic behavior that's relatively easy to obtain and slowly progress in increments to the behavior you want. For example, teaching a dog to touch something with his paw can be shaped to waving good-bye, closing or opening a door, or other behaviors, by clicking at incremental steps until the dog displays the final desired behavior.

specialty A specialized conformation dog show at which only one breed of dog competes.

studbook A list of registered purebred dogs in a breed who were bred and produced puppies.

Organizations

Agility Association of Canada (AAC)
RR #2
Lucan, Ontario
N0N2J0
519-657-7636

AKC Companion Animal Recovery
5580 Centerview Drive, Suite 250
Raleigh, NC 27606-3389
1-800-252-7894
www.akccar.org

American Animal Hospital Association (AAHA)
PO Box 150899
Denver, CO 80215-0899
www.aahanet.org

American College of Veterinary Internal Medicine (ACVIM)
1997 Wadsworth Boulevard, Suite A
Lakewood, CO 80215-3327
www.acvim.org

American Veterinary Medical Association (AVMA)
1931 N. Meacham Road, Suite 100
Schaumburg, IL 60173-4360
847-925-8070
www.avma.org

Canine Eye Registration Foundation
Department of Veterinary Clinical Science
School of Veterinary Medicine
Purdue University
West Lafayette, IN 47907
765-494-8179
Fax: 765-494-9981
www.vet.purdue.edu/~yshen/cerf.html

Cockapoo Club of America
31766 Oak Ranch Court
Westlake Village, CA 91361
www.cockapooclub.com

International Labradoodle Association
Natalie Woods, Registrar
1102 Forest Trail
Cedar Park, TX 78613
www.ilainc.com

National Dog Registry
Box 116
Woodstock, NY 12498
1-800-637-3647
www.natldogregistry.com

North American Cockapoo Registry
400 Birdwalk
Crossville, TN 38572
Fax: 928-395-0800
office@cockapoos.com
www.cockapoos.com

North American Flyball Association, Inc.
1400 W. Devon Avenue, #512
Chicago, IL 60660
309-688-9840
flyball@flyball.org
www.flyball.org

Orthopedic Foundation for Animals
2300 Nifong Boulevard
Columbia, MO 65201
573-442-0418
www.offa.org

Pet Assure
10 South Morris Street
Dover, NJ 07801
1-888-789-PETS (1-888-789-7387)
custserv@petassure.com
www.petassure.com/

Pet Plan Insurance (Canada)
777 Portage Avenue
Winnipeg, MB R3G 0N3 Canada
905-279-7190
www.petplan.com/

PetCare Insurance Programs
PO Box 8575
Rolling Meadows, IL 60008-8575
1-866-275-PETS (1-866-275-7387)
info@petcareinsurance.com
www.petcareinsurance.com/us/

Petshealth Insurance Agency
PO Box 2847
Canton, OH 44720
1-888-592-7387
www.petshealthplan.com/

Premier Pet Insurance Group
9541 Harding Boulevard
Wauwatosa, WI 53226
1-877-774-2273

Tattoo-a-Pet
6571 S.W. 20th Court
Ft. Lauderdale, FL 33317
1-800-828-8667
www.tattoo-a-pet.com

United States Dog Agility Association (USDAA)
PO Box 850955
Richardson, TX 75085-0955
972-231-9700
Information line: 1-888-AGILITY (1-888-244-5489)
info@usdaa.com
www.usdaa.com/

Veterinary Pet Insurance (VPI)
PO Box 2344
Brea, CA 92822-2344
1-800-USA-PETS (1-800-872-7387)
www.petinsurance.com/

Appendix C

Further Reading

Alderton, David. *The Dog Care Manual*. Hauppauge, NY: Barron's Educational Series, 1986.

American Kennel Club. *The Complete Dog Book, Nineteenth Edition, Revised*. Hoboken, NJ: Howell Book House, 1997.

Benjamin, Carol Lea. *Second-Hand Dog*. Hoboken, NJ: Howell Book House, 1988.

Bonham, Margaret H. *An Introduction to Dog Agility*. Hauppauge, NY: Barron's Educational Series, 2000.

———. *The Complete Guide to Mutts*. Hoboken, NJ: Howell Book House, 2004.

———. *The Simple Guide to Getting Active with Your Dog*. Neptune City, NJ: TFH Publications Inc, 2002.

Bonham, Margaret H., and Wingert, James M., D.V.M. *The Complete Idiot's Guide to Dog Health and Nutrition*. Indianapolis: Alpha Books, 2003.

Coffman, Howard D. *The Dry Dog Food Reference*. Nashua, NH: Pig Dog Press, 1995.

Eldredge, Debra, D.V.M. *Pills for Pets: The A to Z Guide to Drugs and Medications for Your Animal Companion*. New York: Citadel Press, 2003.

Fogle, Bruce, D.V.M. *The New Encyclopedia of the Dog*. New York: DK Books, 2000.

Giffin, James M., M.D., and Carlson, Lisa D., D.V.M. *The Dog Owner's Home Veterinary Handbook, Third Edition*. Hoboken, NJ: Howell Book House, 2000.

James, Ruth B., D.V.M. *The Dog Repair Book*. Mills, WY: Alpine Press, 1990.

Klever, Ulrich. *The Complete Book of Dog Care*. Hauppauge, NY: Barron's Educational Series, 1989.

LaBelle, Charlene. *A Guide to Backpacking with Your Dog*. Loveland, CO: Alpine Publications, 1993.

Streitferdt, Uwe. *Healthy Dog, Happy Dog*. Hauppauge, NY: Barron's Educational Series, 1994.

Volhard, Joachim, Wendy Volhard, and Jack Volhard. *The Canine Good Citizen: Every Dog Can Be One*. Hoboken, NJ: Howell Book House, 1997.

You can also check out periodicals, such as the following:

Dog Fancy
PO Box 53264
Boulder, CO 80322-3264
1-800-365-4421
www.dogfancy.com

Index

The Complete Idiot's Guide to Designer Dogs

W–X

Y–Z